Glasgow

In the wake of an unparalleled housing crisis at the end of the Second World War, Glasgow Corporation rehoused the tens of thousands of private tenants who were living in overcrowded and unsanitary conditions in unimproved Victorian slums. Adopting the designs, the materials and the technologies of modernity they built into the sky, developing high-rise estates on vacant sites within the city and on its periphery.

This book uniquely focuses on the people's experience of this modern approach to housing, drawing on oral histories and archival materials to reflect on the long-term narrative and significance of high-rise homes in the cityscape. It positions them as places of identity formation, intimacy and well-being. With discussions on interior design and consumption, gender roles, children, the elderly, privacy, isolation, social networks and nuisance, *Glasgow* examines the connections between architectural design, planning decisions and housing experience to offer some timely and prescient observations on the success and failure of this very modern housing solution at a moment when high flats are simultaneously denigrated in the social housing sector while being built afresh in the private sector.

Glasgow is aimed at an academic readership, including postgraduate students, scholars and researchers. It will be of interest to social, cultural and urban historians particularly interested in the United Kingdom.

Lynn Abrams is Professor of Modern History at the University of Glasgow. Her research focuses on the modern history of gender relations, the practice and theory of oral history and the social and cultural history of modern Scotland.

Ade Kearns is Professor of Urban Studies at the University of Glasgow. He has published widely on housing, neighbourhoods and community cohesion and led the GoWell programme, a long-term study of the impacts of regeneration in Glasgow.

Barry Hazley is Derby Fellow in the Institute of Irish Studies, University of Liverpool and Research Fellow on a project examining Northern Irish migrants during the Troubles in Great Britain. His research focuses on the social and cultural history of modern Britain and Ireland.

Valerie Wright is a historian of modern Britain with expertise in gender, social and political history. She is currently Research Fellow in the Faculty of Social Sciences at the University of Stirling.

Built Environment City Studies

The *Built Environment City Studies* series provides researchers and academics with a detailed look at individual cities through a specific lens. These concise books delve into a case study of an international city, focusing on a key built environment topic. Written by scholars from around the world, the collection provides a library of thorough studies into trends, developments and approaches that affect our cities.

Seville: Through the Urban Void
Miguel Torres

Amman: Gulf Capital, Identity, and Contemporary Megaprojects
Majd Musa

Baltimore: Reinventing an Industrial Legacy City
Klaus Philipsen

Milan: Productions, Spatial Patterns and Urban Change
Edited by Simonetta Armondi and Stefano Di Vita

Baghdad: An Urban History through the Lens of Literature
Iman Al-Attar

Istanbul: Informal Settlements and Generative Urbanism
Noah Billig

Rio de Janeiro: Urban Expansion and Environment
José L. S. Gámez, Zhongjie Lin and Jeffrey S Nesbit

Kuala Lumpur: Community, Infrastructure and Urban Inclusivity
Marek Kozłowski, Asma Mehan and Krzysztof Nawratek

Glasgow: High-Rise Homes, Estates and Communities in the Post-War Period
Lynn Abrams, Ade Kearns, Barry Hazley and Valerie Wright

Glasgow

High-Rise Homes, Estates and
Communities in the Post-War Period

**Lynn Abrams,
Ade Kearns,
Barry Hazley and
Valerie Wright**

Routledge
Taylor & Francis Group

LONDON AND NEW YORK

First published 2020
by Routledge
2 Park Square, Milton Park, Abingdon, Oxon OX14 4RN

and by Routledge
52 Vanderbilt Avenue, New York, NY 10017

Routledge is an imprint of the Taylor & Francis Group, an informa business

© 2020 Lynn Abrams, Ade Kearns, Barry Hazley and Valerie Wright

British Library Cataloguing-in-Publication Data
A catalogue record for this book is available from the British Library

Library of Congress Cataloging-in-Publication Data
Names: Abrams, Lynn, author. | Kearns, Ade, author. | Hazley, Barry, author. | Wright, Valerie (Research assistant) author.
Title: Glasgow : high-rise homes, estates and communities in the post-war period / Lynn Abrams, Barry Hazley, Ade Kearns, Valerie Wright.
Description: Milton Park, Abingdon, Oxon ; New York, NY : Routledge, 2020. Includes bibliographical references and index.
Identifiers: LCCN 2020004605 (print) | LCCN 2020004606 (ebook) | ISBN 9781138317093 (hardback) | ISBN 9780429455339 (ebook)
Subjects: LCSH: Glasgow (Scotland). Corporation. | High-rise apartment buildings–Great Britain–History–20th century. | Housing–Great Britain–History–20th century.
Classification: LCC HD7333.A3 A59 2020 (print) | LCC HD7333.A3 (ebook) | DDC 307.3/3609414409045–dc23
LC record available at https://lccn.loc.gov/2020004605
LC ebook record available at https://lccn.loc.gov/2020004606

ISBN: 978-1-138-31709-3 (hbk)
ISBN: 978-0-429-45533-9 (ebk)

Typeset in Times New Roman
by Wearset Ltd, Boldon, Tyne and Wear

Contents

vi   *Contents*

Figures

All images reproduced by permission of University of Glasgow Archives and Special Collections. The photographs are included in records of the study 'Homes in High Flats', GB248 [DC 127/22b and c].

Acknowledgements

The research for and writing of this book has been a team effort. We would like to thank the Leverhulme Trust for funding a two year interdisciplinary research project bringing together History and Urban Studies at the University of Glasgow on 'Housing, Everyday Life and Wellbeing over the Long Term, *c*.1950–1975' (RPG-2014-014). The aim was to carry out a long-term assessment of the mass relocation of thousands of Glaswegians in the post-war decades, focusing on two case studies: the high-rise estate and the new town. At the heart of the project was a restudy of Pearl Jephcott's high flats research conducted at the University in the 1960s. All her data is stored at the University of Glasgow Archives and we are grateful to the archive staff for their assistance in facilitating our use of a treasure trove of material. In addition to archival materials we conducted our own oral history interviews and gathered additional reminiscences via our Multi-Storey Memories website. We are indebted to all those people who so generously shared their memories in person and online and who offered us such personal insights into the experiences, good and bad, of high-rise living. Our transcribers did a fantastic job translating hours of recordings into readable transcripts. The writing of this book was undertaken by all four members of the project team. Ade Kearns was chiefly responsible for Chapter 1, Lynn Abrams for Chapter 2, Valerie Wright for Chapter 3 and Barry Hazley for Chapter 4. Abrams and Kearns guided and edited the volume as a whole and wrote the Conclusion and Abrams took overall editorial responsibility. The illustrations are all from the High Flats collection at University of Glasgow Archives.

Abbreviations

CDA   Comprehensive Development Area
GCA   Glasgow City Archives
GHA   Glasgow Housing Association
HES   Historic Environment Scotland
MHLG Ministry of Housing and Local Government
NRS   National Records of Scotland
UGA   University of Glasgow Archives

1 Introduction

The fluctuating fortunes of high-rise housing

From the nineteenth century Glasgow had a reputation as the most 'slum-ridden' city of Britain. Its high density of housing was due to the tenement-style which, though capacious in middle-class streets, was for the vast majority of the people made up of poor-quality, one- and two-roomed dwellings, many of which still lacked interior WCs or baths by the 1940s. Despite surges in public housing provision immediately after the First and the Second World Wars, the long-term failure to improve the housing stock had, by the 1950s, created a terrible legacy of overcrowded, unhealthy homes. One solution was the designation of new towns for over-spill homes at East Kilbride (designated 1945) and Cumbernauld (designated 1955). A second solution was four large-scale estates from the 1940s and 50s, encircling the city and comprising mostly low-rise tenement-style housing. A third solution coming in the late 1950s and continuing to be built until the mid-1970s was high-rise flats. Whilst the first and second solutions remain largely in place, many of the towers have been taken down. Widely maligned as unpopular with tenants and impugned with instigating various social ills, this book provides the first comprehensive study of the social experience of high-rise living in the city during this period.

The first feature of Glasgow's encounter with high-rise living was how sudden it was. As late as 1958 Ronald Miller, Professor of Geography at Glasgow University, was dismayed at the low scale and slow pace of Glasgow's much-debated programme of post-war urban redevelopment. 'Rebuilding in the central district is rare', observed Miller, 'and the city is saddled with certain sadly out-of-date equipment, notably most of its trams, street surfaces and ferries'.[1] Just 12 years later, however, Miller could report a dramatic transfiguration, 'broad swathes' having 'been cut through the blocks of Victorian tenements in as bold a manner as ever Hausmann carved up Paris': 'The city which once had a monotonous skyline of four-storey tenements is now punctuated by over a hundred blocks of towers and slabs soaring to 10, 20 and even 31 storeys high.'[2] In place of the worst tenements, prefabs and squatters' camps were scores of high-rise blocks dotted across vacant sites in the city and perched on its periphery, the result of an enthusiastic and some might say hasty and ill-judged embrace of high-rise housing by city officials as the solution to the housing crisis. Between 1950 and 1975 tens of thousands of Glaswegians were rehoused, many of them moving from private rented accommodation to new council flats in high-rise blocks. The city had been transformed with more than 200 high-rise towers – some the highest in Europe at more than 20 storeys – dominating the landscape.

For Miller and many of his contemporaries, the arrival of Glasgow's high-rise revolution marked an epic moment in the city's history.[3] Where mass housing was widely acknowledged as a source of shame in the city's industrial past, the multi-storey flat symbolised a new era of technological and social progress, heralding unprecedented levels of domestic convenience, comfort and efficiency for Glasgow's long-suffering working-class citizens. Yet even as Miller was writing, a counter-narrative was already in circulation, as part of which the city's embrace of modernism was reinterpreted as a catastrophe waiting to happen.[4]

High-rise housing in Glasgow was the outcome of a combination of factors: the urgent need for new housing; hubris on the part of some politicians and officials at how quickly the housing problem could be fixed; and a utopian vision for communities and families as it was set out by planners, architects and designers in their blueprints, housing designs, community plans and public (and off-record) pronouncements.[5] Though many other cities across the UK also saw high rise as the solution to the post-war housing crisis, Glasgow embraced the tower block with greater verve than anywhere in the post-war decades, building 'goliaths', towers high even by continental standards.[6] Glasgow's housing pattern was distinctive in the UK owing to an amalgamation of factors but principally a legacy of intensely overcrowded, private rental slum housing, which was replaced from the mid twentieth century by an unusually large public housing sector that accounted for as much as 70 per cent of homes by 1970, and that still, in 2018, accommodated 34 per cent of the city's households. This figure contrasts with the Scottish average of 23 per cent and 17 per cent for England.[7] The huge demand for new homes in the post-war years necessitated an embrace of modern mass housing on a monumental scale characterised by overspill, sprawl and high-rise blocks mostly on gap sites and the urban edges. By the first decade of the twenty-first century, around 10 per cent of the city's housing stock – over 30,000 dwellings – comprised high-rise flats. But the city's approach to its housing crisis was also nationally influential as it harnessed the modernist impulse to build homes with a contemporary aesthetic using new (largely untested) building materials and techniques.

The consequences of this housing experiment, which had its greatest impact on social tenants, have not been subject to either serious or extended investigation from social historians.[8] After a flurry of social science research from the community studies school into relocation and new housing solutions from the late 1950s,[9] historians' point of departure, as Richard Rodger remarks in his survey of twentieth century Scottish housing, is 'too frequently the housing stock, new building and other quantifiable variables' rather than "community relations, neighbourhood issues and residents' reactions to housing provision'.[10] Treatments of twentieth century housing in Scotland have privileged political policy and macro-economic processes in shaping post-war modernisation and housing mobility and the alleged long-run negative economic and social consequences of these.[11] These consequences are said to be manifested in the 'Glasgow effect', shorthand for the longstanding excess mortality rates to be found in the Glasgow conurbation and often linked to poor housing conditions amongst other factors.[12] In Glasgow, as one child of a multi-storey estate recently remarked, high-rise social housing 'is synonymous with deprivation', and it left a damaging legacy.[13]

The centenary of the Addison Act of 1919 which paved the way for large scale council-house building in the UK, and the twenty-first century housing crisis, led to the rediscovery of social housing by historians and public commentators from the perspective of policy, design and lived experience.[14] This latest academic trend fosters a range of themes, from the celebration and condemnation of brutalist architecture, the critique of public housing policy, to in-depth studies of towns and estates which challenge perceptions of working-class suburbia. Yet the experience of those who lived in social housing of all types has hardly been addressed and high-rise living least of all. Greater attention has been paid to the architecture of the tower block than the people who resided there.[15] Lynsey Hanley's autobiographically-inflected account of council housing in Britain is one of the few studies which does place the personal within the wider political and policy context but it pursues a failure narrative in which council housing estates have come to act as 'ciphers for a malingering society than as places where people actually live'.[16] Works such as John Boughton's celebration of the values inherent in the idea of the council estate in which he argues that council housing represents a now largely lost sense of the importance of decency, and Ravetz's cultural history of council housing, seek to reveal its place in the history of twentieth century working-class life and offer accounts which pay attention to both the aspirations of those who planned and designed estates and those whose material conditions markedly improved when they gained a tenancy. Yet neither engages specifically or deeply with the experience of those who moved to high-rise housing which, we argue, was a materially distinctive experience from low rise.[17] This book, with its long perspective and in-depth focus on experience, shifts the perspective towards those who matter the most, the residents.

Despite its status then as one of the most controversial episodes in British housing history, the embrace of high rise has been studied almost solely – with the exception of architectural history – in terms of its decline and failure, what we might describe as the utopianism gone bad narrative. A significant proportion of those people living in social housing in urban areas since the 1960s were housed in a tower block, but little of this experience has been subjected to scrutiny. Such has been the power of the simplistic 'design failure' paradigm with which high-rise blocks have been viewed retrospectively, that the experiential dimensions of high-rise living have rarely been addressed in all their complexity.[18]

By contrast, contemporary housing studies research is actively and deeply engaged in seeking to understand present day housing experiences in order to inform local and national housing policy. High-rise housing has featured prominently in analyses of contemporary housing issues in the UK and in Scotland in particular, demonstrating that outcomes for people living in high rise tend to be worse than for those in other forms of social housing.[19] Following the influential studies of Jacobs and Newman in the Unites States and Coleman in the UK which argued that the design features of high-rise estates had a significant negative effect on 'social malaise', recent analysis has produced more nuanced assessments of the relationship between high rise and wellbeing across a wide range of indicators including social contact, mental and physical health, and crime.[20] In Glasgow an extensive study of house occupants comparing high rise and other forms of flatted living concluded that residents of tower blocks experienced poorer outcomes in respect of security, noise and the physical condition of their homes. Moreover, residents of high rise were 'less likely than people elsewhere to derive recuperative psychosocial benefits of the home such as privacy, safety, and retreat …' on account of poor community cohesion, low levels of social contact and weak social support networks. The study concluded that high-rise housing 'offers greater challenges than other dwelling types' for 'relatively deprived individuals and communities'.[21] These are important findings in the light of some recent calls to reconsider high rise as the answer to future social housing needs.[22]

Research into contemporary housing issues tends, however, to focus on the short-term perspective. Yet, there is value in taking the long view. The idea of this book – that context can be historical – that is, the placing of large-scale developments within a longer time frame of social and economic change – as well as social and spatial, is a new departure in looking at this twentieth century housing policy experiment. Excavating people's experience of high rise from the early years of this form of housing reveals a very different landscape from that which exists today. Listening to the housing stories of former and current occupants of high-rise flats juxtaposes memories embedded in the 1960s and 1970s, when rehousing to a multi-storey was for many a dream come true or at least a marked improvement in their material conditions, with reflections on high-rise living shaped by the intervening years when many estates were beset by social and material problems. Thus, the long view does two things: it permits us to offer a more informed and nuanced understanding of how, when and why some estates failed; and it contributes to debates about the place of high-rise housing in the present.

What follows is a novel but realistic evaluation of the high-rise experiment in Glasgow between the late 1950s and the present which places the views and memories of residents centre stage. This book focuses on the people's experience of this modern approach to housing, drawing on oral histories and archival materials including the first serious research project on high rise undertaken in the UK, social scientist Pearl Jephcott's High Flats study which analysed Glasgow's high-rise experience between 1966 and 1969.[23] We cross the threshold to enter the homes of those who lived in high flats in the city and on its periphery to consider these homes as places of identity formation, intimacy and wellbeing. With discussions of interior design and consumption, gender roles, children, the elderly, privacy, isolation, the environment, social networks and nuisance, and working from the inside out, this book examines the connections between architectural design, planning decisions and housing experience and offers some timely observations on the success and failure of this very modern housing solution at a moment when high flats are almost universally denigrated in the social housing sector while being built afresh in the private sector.

Walking around Glasgow today, one might not appreciate the sheer audacity of the building programme that transformed the city in the 1960s and 1970s. Following piecemeal demolitions in the 1990s, in 2006 Glasgow City Council announced a 'revolution in house-building', a large-scale demolition, refurbishment and re-housing programme. Many of the highest and some of the most reviled high-rise blocks have been demolished over the years, including Basil Spence's design for Queen Elizabeth Square in the Gorbals and the Red Road flats, famous for their height but renowned for the hostile environment the blocks incubated in their later years. Other blocks have been refurbished as part of a city-wide regeneration programme. However, despite the disappearance of many tower blocks, memories of high-rise living are still vivid. In this book we mine the personal stories of former high-rise residents, many of whom moved to a high flat in the pioneer decades, the 1960s and 1970s, and consider their testimonies alongside reports gathered shortly after people had moved in when reactions to the new homes were still fresh. But first we describe Glasgow's relationship with high rise between the 1950s and the present day, accounting for the embrace of this style of housing in the early decades, the subsequent retreat in the 1970s and 1980s and finally demolition and partial revival in the 1990s and 2000s.

Embracing high rise in the post-war period

Glasgow built its first high-rise flats at the start of the 1950s. Crathie Court in Partick, an eight-storey block of one-bedroom flats opened in 1952. This was followed by the larger Moss Heights development in Cardonald comprising three 10-storey blocks of flats for families, constructed between 1950 and 1954. These early experiments – Crathie Court was housing for single women, known locally as the 'spinsters' skyscraper'[24] and Moss Heights was high-spec modern housing ('luxury flats') for the respectable working or lower middle classes – were followed by high-rise mass production, so that by 1975, some 20 years later, Glasgow had 30,396 dwellings in high-rise buildings of six or more storeys.[25] This whole-hearted embrace of new technology and a new built form, referred to as 'the multistorey crash-drive of Glasgow', can be explained by some factors common to many British cities and to housing and architecture in general at this time, and by other issues unique to Glasgow or given a particular inflexion in the case of Scotland's largest city.[26]

First and foremost, Glasgow had a shortage of good quality housing for its citizens in the period after the Second World War. A planning report at the end of the war identified that a large proportion of the city's tenemental housing would not last much longer due to being obsolete and structurally unsound as Figure 1.1 illustrates.[27] The level of amenities in this type of housing was extremely poor; for example 22 per cent of Glasgow's population had no internal WC.[28] Overcrowding was also severe: the city had the highest ratio of persons per room (1.27) than any British city outside London, with a very high percentage of its residents (47 per cent) living in one or two-room dwellings.[29] It was estimated that 80,000 houses were required to adequately house those who required to be cleared from the slums.[30]

By replacing the worst homes, the city expected to see returns in terms of reduced health expenditure and lower juvenile delinquency.[31] The 1951

Figure 1.1 Tenement housing in Glasgow showing washing drying and children playing in the back court.

City Development Plan identified 29 Comprehensive Development Areas (CDAs) to be declared in the city, with a total of 100,000 slum dwellings to be cleared. Indeed, subsequently, Glasgow cleared more of its 1951 housing stock, 40 per cent, than other comparable British cities.[32] However, this level of housing need and rate of demolition does not explain why Glasgow built more high-rise flats than other cities: from 1945 to 1975, 27 per cent of Glasgow's housing production was high-rise dwellings, compared with 25 per cent in Birmingham, 22 per cent in Leeds and less than 20 per cent in other cities; this included 16 per cent of construction being dwellings in very tall buildings of 20 storeys or more, four times the rate in any other city.[33]

If the level of housing need and requirement for housing replacement cannot alone explain the significant advent of high rise in Glasgow, what other factors were in play? Initially, like other cities and several London boroughs, Glasgow built relatively low-rise, typically four-storey modern tenements in the inter-war and immediate post-war period: the city's peripheral estates such as Castlemilk and Drumchapel built in the early 1950s comprised mostly this form of housing. However, by the late 1950s and 1960s Glasgow had turned to high-rise housing in a big way, a change of attitude also observed in other cities such as Birmingham.[34] Several factors prompting this move can be identified: the politics of planning and the perceived lack of space in the city; the attractions of modernism as a design solution and mode of production, which offered speed to match the urgency of housing need; encouragement and facilitation by contractors and through generous government subsidies; and the leadership of individuals.

The post-war planning profession in the UK in the 1940s and 1950s has been described as anti-urbanist and anti-municipal, opposing the power and influence of large, urban housing authorities. Planners favoured garden cities and lower density, mixed-use development in newly planned settlements.[35] A combination of enforcement of green belt policies which prevented cities from acquiring suburban land for expansion development, and the creation of new towns beyond the green belt, advanced the planners' preferred policy of population dispersal though 'overspill'. In Glasgow's case, the approach of the planners was endorsed in two key documents. The Clyde Valley Regional Plan of 1945 (Abercrombie Plan) was approved by the Government in opposition to the City Council's own Glasgow Development Plan (Bruce Plan) of the same year. The Abercrombie Plan proposed that over a quarter of Glasgow's population (250–300,000 people) be moved to beyond the city boundary in order to reduce congestion and relocated into a series of new towns yet to be developed. A decade later, Glasgow's own planners, finding it increasingly difficult to access green belt land, secured approval for a report which confined new build housing within the city to the CDAs, alongside a substantial proportion of overspill as a result of slum clearance.[36]

It was in large part as a response to this perceived 'land trap' that Glasgow's councillors increasingly adopted high-rise solutions as the 1950s moved into the 1960s.[37] As well as the potential greater loss of population in the absence of any alternative to overspill, Glasgow councillors were also faced with a shortage of money and land. The city had high debt, low incomes, a low-rent policy, and a small owner-occupied housing sector, which meant its rental and rateable incomes were low, particularly in comparison to the redevelopment task it faced at the time.[38] Further, due to a mixture of hilly or poor terrain, the need for industrial development and road building, plus the green belt constraints, land for large housing developments was generally in short supply. Thus, the choice of slender point-block high-rise buildings was better suited to the use of small, gap sites within the city. Figure 1.2 is a pictoral illustration of the distribution of high flat sites across the city by 1969. This policy was pursued in order to combat overspill and, according to commentators such as Glendinning and Muthesius, as a counter to the planners' preference for larger,

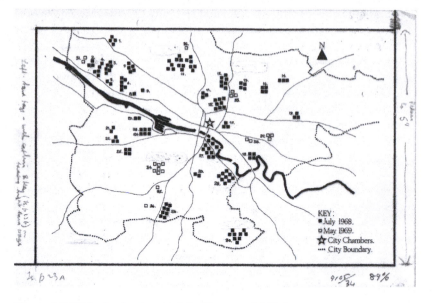

Figure 1.2 High-rise developments in Glasgow, 1968–9.

Source: map produced by Pearl Jephcott for the 'Homes in High Flats' project.

holistically planned schemes; they described the multi-storey block as 'a weapon tailor-made for a defensive building campaign'.[39] The use of this 'output weapon' resulted in Glasgow having 163 high-rise blocks in occupation by 1969 by which time the city was building six high-rise flats to every one low-rise dwelling.[40]

High-rise building also had other attractions. The city's peripheral estates of modern tenements were coming in for criticism on the grounds of location, monotony, and lack of facilities, so that an alternative form of provision became attractive to local politicians.[41] On hilly sites, or in close proximity to industry, roads or railways, high blocks offered the opportunity to raise people up into the light and air, which was an influential consideration following the poor environments of the inner-city slums. High-rise enabled the city planners to achieve high densities and a scale of output that suited their purpose of population retention and rateable value enhancement within the city boundaries. With scattered sites available, high-rise developments could be assembled into packages that achieved a higher rate of production. 'Off-the-shelf' high-rise designs from contractors such as Wimpey and John Laing via package deals (where the contractor designed, built and supervised the development) alongside design and construction undertaken by Glasgow Corporation's Direct Labour force, offered a speed of production and certainty of cost that were lacking in architect-designed developments. Difficulties with the latter were experienced at one of the earliest CDAs to be redeveloped in Glasgow, Gorbals Hutchesontown, designed by the architects Sir Robert Matthew and Sir Basil Spence. Of these large developments, the verdict was that 'the output usefulness of these schemes was vitiated by slowness and cost overruns'.[42] The construction of Spence's design for Queen Elizabeth Square in the Gorbals by Cubit is a prime example of a prestige project which cost more than estimated and experienced considerable delays with a spokesperson for the constructors opining in exasperation:

> People must decide whether they want council flats built quickly or whether they want monuments of architecture. Do they want houses or do they want other people to point and say 'look! There is a block of flats built by so-and-so.'[43]

As well as providing (for the most part) speed and certainty in construction, finance for building was also important. The Hutchesontown CDA was approved in 1957, a year after the Housing Subsidies Act 1956, which introduced government subsidies for local authority council house construction that varied by storey height. The Ministry of Housing and Local Government (MHLG) had received evidence that, rather than being cheaper due to higher densities and therefore lower land acquisition costs, construction costs per dwelling increased with storey height.[44] The 1956 legislation therefore increased the exchequer subsidy per dwelling in blocks of four, five and six storeys, with a uniform increase per storey above that. As a result, a flat in a 20-storey block could receive a subsidy seven times that for a general needs dwelling or three-and-a-half times the subsidy for a slum clearance dwelling in a building of three storeys or less. This subsidy system is often described as having encouraged local authorities to build high-rise flats (and was important in a city like Glasgow facing financial challenges due to population loss) at least until the Housing Subsidies Act 1967 which removed the subsidy multiplier above six storeys. The average density of local authority housing construction (a proxy for building height) peaked in 1966–8.[45]

Building large numbers of high-rise blocks within the city can also be seen as a political response by the city's leaders to their perceived defenestration by planners who were facilitating the depopulation of the city to the surrounding new towns. This was both a numbers game and an issue of image and reputation, bringing together the forces of modernism and political muscle. Local politicians, in the face of the overspill movement, were keen to preserve and demonstrate their autonomy and to showcase their cities as powerful with optimistic futures, rather than being associated with the poor conditions of the past and facing a future of decline. Embracing modernism in the form of high-rise enabled them to do this. Thus high buildings offered both 'their suitability for high output and their visual connotation of modernity and progress'.[46] Indeed, prior to deciding how to proceed with its CDAs, a Glasgow City Council delegation visited the emblem of modernist housing, Le Corbusier's 17-storey development of 300 flats, Unité d'Habitation, in Marseille in 1954, as did other British local authorities at the time.[47]

The report from the Marseille visit raised a number of concerns about the development, most of which were either ignored or refuted by the delegates upon their return, including: that it would be unsuitable to Glasgow's colder, wet climate; it was very expensive to construct (witness the later cost overruns on some sites); the sheer scale would not allow households to 'get away from one another'; and that such a building would not be suitable for letting to slum dwellers.[48] This last observation is hard to decipher but it may have been a recognition of the potential vulnerability of the building to damage if not used in accordance with the designer's intentions.[49] Despite these concerns, Glasgow City Council approved a design for Hutchesontown 'C' that was similar in many ways to Le Corbusier's development, and of course, proceeded to build high-rise flats across the city for the next 20 years.

The key individuals identified as responsible for pushing the city's progress with high rise include the Housing Committee Convenor, Councillor David Gibson, the City Engineer, Lewis Cross, and the architect Sam Bunton who had a background in designing large housing schemes in the 1940s and whose practice, Sam Bunton & Associates, designed the Red Road development in 1962. Gibson, whose epitaph was 'written in hundreds of multi-storey houses and homes' and in the naming of Gibson Heights, a 13-storey block in the Drygate area of Glasgow, was often portrayed as a zealot for high rise, criticised and praised in equal measure.[50] As a labour councillor he championed the housing needs of Glasgow's poor and saw high rise as the solution within the city, riding rough-shod over the opposition and managing to persuade even the city's golfers that they would have to sacrifice their greens to housing.[51] In a press interview Gibson was reported as saying: 'My idea of fulfilment is to draw up the car and see the lights of Knightswood or some other scheme shining out and think of all the families translated from gloom to happiness.' The report added: 'Glasgow ... has 12,000 cesspots of housing. He dreams, in the odour of bone, fat and blood of getting rid of them all.'[52] Given the delays with large, fully designed schemes like Gorbals Hutchesontown, these individuals and the city corporation preferred rapid production of high-rise blocks on smaller gap sites. The authorities were said to have become less interested in issues of community preservation, mixed development comprising different types of building, and the provision of a range of amenities, as they become more energised by the speed and scale of housing production at lower cost.

Retreat from high rise

By the early 1970s, the high-rise building boom was over across the UK. The proportion of public sector dwelling construction comprising high flats (in blocks of five storeys or more) reached a peak of 50 per cent in 1966 and declined thereafter, and was below 20 per cent from 1971 onwards.[53] Approvals for flats in very high blocks (15 storeys or more) fell from 11 per cent in 1966 to zero by 1976.[54] By the mid-1970s, when high-rise construction in the public housing sector ceased, there were 321 high-rise blocks in the city owned by the Council and Scottish Special Housing Association (SSHA).[55] There are a number of reasons for the retreat from high rise in the 1970s and 80s, starting with costs and finances.

As indicated, analysis had revealed that high-rise construction was more expensive than low rise and housing subsidies had been adjusted in 1956 to reflect this. At the same time, the introduction of the Parker Morris standards for space and heating in 1969 did not make construction any cheaper. Along with the advent of the Housing Cost Yardstick of 1967, which limited government subsidies and loan sanctions to house building schemes falling within specified cost parameters, the housing finance system for council housing was changed in the late 1960s in ways which discouraged local authorities from building costlier high-rise buildings. The late 1960s and early 1970s were also a time of increasing costs for the repair, maintenance and management of council housing alongside what has been described as a 'chaotic' and 'confused system of public housing finance'.[56] Faced with such realities it is not surprising that Glasgow like other local authorities (but particularly given Glasgow's preference for low council rents) withdrew from high-rise construction when the incentives and advantages became uncertain, and evidence of problems with high rise were increasing.

The advance of high rise was also halted because the need for it, associated with slum clearance, that is the 'high density demands of redevelopment', dissipated.[57] During the 1960s, slum clearance and 'comprehensive redevelopment came under increased attack at a technical and social level'.[58] The social costs of slum clearance had been highlighted by studies in London and Bristol, including the reported break-up of working class communities and the isolating effects of relocation to suburban developments.[59] A debate also took place in the late 1960s on the comparative costs of redevelopment versus rehabilitation, commencing in academia[60] and eventually being reflected in government guidance which encouraged a cost-benefit analysis of the two approaches to tackling poor housing conditions.[61] Whilst there was a debate about how well the CDA formulations took into account the various parameters in favour of one approach or the other, nevertheless this new requirement reflected the fact that clearance and redevelopment were no longer assumed to be the correct approach.

A retreat from redevelopment was also prompted by realisation of the scale of the problem. The first national house condition survey of 1967 showed that over six million dwellings were in need of repairs or basic amenities, with around a million homes requiring demolition.[62] This would necessitate a substantial, increased and ongoing clearance programme costing a significant amount of public money, while still leaving a large proportion of the housing stock in an unsatisfactory condition. The sheer cost of enacting sufficient clearance against the backdrop of a balance of payments crisis in 1967 prompted a rethink. There were also concerns for the blighting effects of declaring clearance areas that took a long time to progress, and that clearance areas increasingly included housing that could be saved. There was therefore a shift in housing policy from clearance and redevelopment (via high flats) to the rehabilitation of the existing inner-city housing stock. This shift was presaged in the 1968 White Paper *Old Houses into New Homes* and implemented through the Housing Acts of 1969 and 1974.

But it was not costs alone that caused a withdrawal from high-rise construction by councils. From the early days of high rise and through the 1970s and 80s, high rise was identified as problematic for families and for vulnerable individuals. In addition, the buildings themselves were found to be susceptible to damage and the estates of which they formed part (as well as other low-rise estates) were considered deficient. High-rise flats were not initially intended for families; some blocks were explicitly designed for singletons such as Crathie Court in Partick, while others were deemed suitable for the elderly, yet many families were allocated to live in them. Early concerns were expressed about where children would play, and about their social development, while later studies identified behavioural problems and learning difficulties among children living in high flats.[63]

In Glasgow, Pearl Jephcott found that 27 per cent of the households in high flats contained children under the age of 16, and reported that the tenants in the study 'universally agreed that a high flat was not a good home for children'.[64] Jephcott expressed concerns for the physical and social limitations placed upon children by living in high-rise homes – to be considered further in Chapter 3 – and recommended that high flats should not be allocated to families with primary school and pre-school age children. The same study identified that high flats 'made problems for mothers', portending subsequent studies of mental health that found that mothers with several school age children who lived in high flats were more at risk of depression than others,[65] that adults with a 'neurotic personality' were vulnerable to feelings of isolation and loneliness in high flats, and that living in high flats 'seems hazardous and stressful for certain vulnerable, disadvantaged groups'.[66]

A decade after Jephcott's study was published, Glasgow City Council recognised that there were problems for families in high-rise flats, without explicitly acknowledging its own role in bringing this about:

> Multi-storey flats were first designed to house families without children, at least above the fourth floor. However, the pressure of demand for housing forced multi-storey living on an increasing number of young occupants for whom there was no other alternative. Recognising the problems of multi-storey living as a way of life for families with young children, Council is considering new approaches in making such accommodation more acceptable for present occupants, and modifying allocation policies to bring households without children to the multi-storeys.[67]

One of Jephcott's other observations on families in high flats, which would be seen as condescending from today's perspective, nonetheless contains a kernel of truth about the vulnerability not only of the residents but also of high-rise buildings themselves:

> High flats are likely to include some ... families [who bear the marks of generations of deprivation]; and it is asking a lot of them suddenly to show the self-restraint, social competence and rather nice habits needed for a satisfactory use of multi-storey housing.[68]

High-rise developments were found in practice to suffer faults, to be vulnerable to damage, and to have high repair costs. Industrialised building techniques, whether prefabricated or made of concrete cast on site, were subject to 'jerry-building', 'shoddy manufacturing', and poor assembly, so that design flaws were exacerbated.[69] The collapse of Ronan Point in London in 1968 following a gas explosion in an eighteenth-floor flat emphasised something that became increasingly evident, namely that 'system-built' could also mean systematically defective. The observations of the Hulme estate in Manchester (a system-built, six-storey, mass housing estate) could have been applied to many modernist estates with and without tower blocks, namely that 'structural flaws and design issues were rapidly compounded ... by [the council's] failure to fulfil basic tasks of maintenance and upkeep'.[70] Such lack of investment and upkeep would not have encouraged residents' respect for their immediate environment and likely exacerbated the vulnerability of the buildings.

In the late 1960s, in her survey of around 1,000 residents' views on high flat living in Glasgow, Pearl Jephcott focused especially on the disadvantages of insufficient numbers, size and speed of lifts in high-rise buildings, and the frequency and duration of lift breakdowns. These early observations about lifts – in particular the extremely poor service at the 31-storey Red Road flats was highlighted – proved prescient. By the early 1980s, the City Council was spending £1.72 million per year on maintaining the 539 lifts in its high-rise buildings.[71] Other resident complaints related to clothes drying facilities, lighting, rubbish chutes, emergency exit doors etc.; many of these things were inadequate, subject to accidental damage, or vulnerable to criminal damage, antisocial behaviour and misuse. The buildings were also susceptible to the poor weather in Scotland, something warned about in the early days after the Marseille visit. By the early 1980s, the City Council declared that it 'Views dampness as one of Glasgow's most serious housing problems.... At least 35,000 of Glasgow's council dwellings are affected' and that 'Dampness is particularly prevalent in those non-traditionally built dwellings constructed in the sixties and seventies'.[72] A Glasgow City Council house condition survey of 1985 reported that 80 per cent of dwellings in tower blocks built after 1964 in the city required repairs to external elements to prevent penetrating damp, a third suffered condensation or dampness, and one-in-ten post-1964 high-rise dwellings had mould in more than one room.[73] Repairing the faults with high rise causing dampness was costing the council money, as was the lost rental income: in 1982, nearly one-in-10 council dwellings in the central city area was empty with 'the high total due to dampness in Hutchesontown',[74] the once-lauded, architect-designed high-rise development of the 1960s described as the 'miracle in the Gorbals'.[75]

Not only the buildings themselves, but the estates of which they were part came to be seen as problematic. In the first flush of enthusiasm for high flats in Glasgow the emphasis had been on building new homes as quickly as possible; the amenities, especially for those located in the remoter areas, were to come later. But the provision of shops, playgrounds, doctor's surgeries and even public telephones, was slow to materialise in some estates. The lack of amenities and the associated absence of footfall and opportunities for everyday social interaction led to criticisms of boredom and monotony, and accusations that the design of the modernist, mostly tall, buildings and of the estates themselves, caused or at the very least facilitated, crime and antisocial behaviour. For their critics, from Oscar Newman's work in New York to Alice Coleman's investigations in the UK, high-rise estates were associated with high levels of crime, due to insufficiencies in territorial influence and natural surveillance; the buildings and estates offered opportunities for crime to take place out of sight, and for the perpetrators to go undetected, referred to by Coleman as 'design disadvantagement'.[76]

Coleman's work has been heavily criticised methodologically, mainly for not taking into account the population size of different blocks in associating higher crime with tall buildings, and ideologically, for ignoring the effects of poverty or as one commentator put it, for 'positively disdaining it' and thus 'invalidating' her 'architectural determinism'.[77] However, both Coleman's work and that of Anne Power were influential upon Conservative Governments of the 1980s and 90s as attention was focused on 'unpopular council estates' and 'difficult to let housing' which was monitored by government from 1978 onwards and found to be concentrated in large, modern housing estates.[78] In Scotland, 46 'Low Demand Public Sector Estates' were identified by the housing agency Scottish Homes in the early 1990s.[79]

The problems of high rise and of the estates of which they formed part were compounded by the gradual residualisation of council housing in the UK. Residualisation refers to the changing role of social housing, identified from the late 1970s onwards and involving public housing being an 'ambulance service' for people with a range of special needs[80] or as a 'safety net' for those who cannot find housing elsewhere.[81] Thus it results in a changing tenant composition within the social housing sector, but also a reduction in status, investment, scale and housing stock quality. With residualisation, social housing becomes less socially and politically relevant as it experiences policy and physical decline, resulting in the stigmatisation of the tenure.[82] Residualisation has been attributed to various government policies, including the Conservative Government's 1972 Housing Finance Act which raised council rents and reduced subsidies to council housing with 'the intention ... to increase pressure on better-off tenants to move out and become home owners' as part of a 'determined effort to confine council housing to a residual role'.[83] The following Labour Government's 1977 Housing (Homeless Persons) Act further contributed to this trend by requiring councils to rehouse particular vulnerable groups with priority needs such as families, pregnant women and people with health issues.[84]

Others, however, have argued that residualisation also reflected the fact that the effects of economic decline and public expenditure cuts were concentrated in the council sector in terms of unemployment and reductions in welfare benefits to tenants.[85] Residualisation was also evident in a contracting council housing sector, and in Glasgow at this time, council house production fell by three-quarters from 1976 to 1981 (from 1,900 dwellings per annum to 558)[86] and the total council housing stock reduced by around 20,000 dwellings from 1975 to 1985 (from 183,458 dwellings to 165,057).[87] At the same time, by 1983 two-thirds of those council house lettings which were made to the homeless, and half of the lettings made to those on the housing waiting list, were made to single persons under retirement age or to single parents.[88] Moreover, an analysis of council house lettings at the time revealed that a much higher proportion of those people allocated houses in the least popular areas of the city were on very low incomes, something explained by the use of the least popular areas to house homeless people, and by those on lower incomes having less ability to exercise choice within the housing system. The city's low status areas were identified as those with high-rise and modern tenemental flats, with the very least popular areas being the city's large, peripheral housing estates – Easterhouse, Drumchapel and Castlemilk – which contained a significant proportion of high flats.[89]

Undoubtedly, poor performance by local authorities combined with financial constraints placed on council housing budgets contributed to the unpopularity of much council housing. The circumstances of Scottish council housing in the 1980s have been attributed to a number of factors, including a long-term failure to maintain the stock, particularly where 'relatively non-traditional stock has deteriorated at an alarming rate at early vintages'.[90] In the less popular areas, there was said to be resident dissatisfaction with both housing conditions and neighbourhood conditions, and a lack of awareness by councils that people would demand higher quality environments as their incomes rose.[91] Not only did most councils in Scotland at the time lack a long-term planned maintenance strategy, but in Glasgow three-quarters of tenants were dissatisfied with the council's repairs service[92] with less than one-quarter (24 per cent) of the council's Housing Revenue Account income in 1984/5 being spent on repairs, the majority (63 per cent) going to loan charges to pay for the post-war construction boom.[93]

Residualisation is said to have created an image (and to a large extent a reality) of council housing as being a social service only for the most needy. With the growing popularity of owner occupation from the late 1970s onwards, most people with economic power and choice opted for alternative housing tenures. Within the social housing sector, the identification of welfare housing for an 'underclass' was focused particularly on large, especially modernist-designed council housing estates of poor quality.[94] As Boughton puts it, there was 'a broader assault against not merely the form of council estates, but the concept'.[95] In design terms, this was reflected in a shift away from modernism towards more conservative designs sympathetic to local historic forms. The fortunes of council housing and of high rise were also tied up with a shift in political and ideological terms. There was a growing aversion to modernism as a movement and utopianism as a social ideal, and as the 1970s moved into the 1980s, the political mood in Britain shifted further from socialism towards conservatism so that 'utopian' became a term of abuse.[96]

Thus, from building *modernist* high-rise estates in the 1950s, 60s and 70s, the UK government now moved through a series of attempts to *modernise* such estates in the 1980s and 90s. Three central government initiatives followed one after the other in England: Priority Estates Project in 1979, Estate Action in 1985 and Housing Action Trusts in 1988. In Scotland, similar initiatives were launched: New Life for Urban Scotland (1988), and Priority Partnership Areas (1995). These programmes, or ones similar, affected Glasgow's council estates as others, and involved a mixture of design modifications (including reductions in storey height for tall buildings and the removal of elevated walkways between blocks), localised management and maintenance, tenant involvement, diversification of the ownership and management of estates through sales or transfers to charitable trusts and private developers, and housing tenure diversification through a variety of subsidised home ownership schemes. Under these approaches and in this period high-rise flats were mostly retained and improved, through repairs and some remodelling. The Council also sought to find alternative uses for some of its tower blocks by converting some of them to sheltered housing with community spaces, wardens and intercom systems, and using others in due course for specific groups such as students, nurses and asylum seekers.

Removal and return of high rise

In 1982, Glasgow City Council felt confident to declare that 'there is no possibility of (nor is there a need for) a long-term return to the days of massive housing demolition programmes'.[97] This was mainly a comment on the end of the slum clearance programmes of the 1950s and 60s and the growing policy emphasis upon housing rehabilitation. However, the statement proved to be an inaccurate prediction as regards high-rise council housing. Twenty years later, housing stock transfer in Glasgow, whereby the city council's housing was transferred into the ownership of an independent social landlord, was followed by a large-scale planned demolition programme of 'excess' social housing, a large proportion of which comprised multi-storey flats. This happened against the background of attempting to provide tenants with better quality housing (with the worst housing taken out of the picture), and in the context of long-term decline in the demand for social housing.[98]

One of the objectives of housing stock transfer was to deliver a sustainable housing system within the city. Glasgow Housing Association (GHA) translated this objective to mean (among other things) that social housing, and specifically that which GHA managed, should be 'Of the quality, type and location that people want' and 'Capable of being managed and maintained at reasonable costs and without substantial further injections of public money, for at least another 20 years'.[99] One of the reasons for the second of these criteria was the second stage transfer process, whereby GHA was due to pass on the stock to community-led organisations in due course, and wanted to ensure that in doing so, the housing would be free of 'unforeseen costs and performance issues [that] will put the business in trouble'.[100] This meant disposing of the least sustainable stock after a process of 'housing future assessments'. GHA assumed that within its first ten years it would demolish 14,000 of the 80,500 dwellings it acquired through transfer; only 'housing stock with a long-term future, which is sufficiently safe to justify substantial investment' was to be retained.[101] Three years after stock transfer, GHA's asset management strategy identified nearly three-fifths (58 per cent) of its remaining housing stock (approximately 23,000 dwellings out of 74,000) as multi-storey flats. Housing demand projections commissioned by GHA indicated that in ten years' time it might own more social housing than there was demand for in the city and that 'there is a demand risk attaching to a significant proportion of MSF [multi-storey flat] stock ...'.[102] While multi-storey flats accounted for 58 per cent of the organisation's housing stock, only 16 per cent of those on GHA's waiting list, and 8 per cent of its transfer applicants, wanted a multi-storey flat.[103] Accordingly, by 2006 GHA planned to demolish approximately 14,700 multi-storey flats, with 8,140 being retained.

Such large-scale demolition has not been without its critics or opponents, although for the most part demolition has proceeded as intended including Basil Spence's Queen Elizabeth Square development in 1993 and the Red Road flats between 2012 and 2015. There have been instances of local opposition to the demolition of particular tower blocks as well as a wider movement expressing regret at the loss of the city's modernist and high-rise past. Although some of the problems associated with high-rise living are well documented by research and recognised by critics in passing – including crime and antisocial behaviour, negative impacts on families with children, and mental and physical health effects – it is also argued that such 'modernist gems' should be protected against demolition and ensuing gentrification.[104] Architectural historians contend that although 'dismissed as ugly', modernist buildings including tower blocks are 'impressive architectural constructions with great ideas' that 'helped to bring communities together' (at least in the post-war period), and above all were 'affordable housing structures'.[105]

For local artists such as Chris Leslie, the demolition programme provided an opportunity for social documentary, photographing the emptied, dismantled towers and interviewing past residents, many of whom identified causes of the towers' decline, including changes in the council's allocation of properties to house vulnerable tenants in tower blocks, the arrival of drug dealing and use of heroin, and the passing of modernist fashion.[106] Reporting that 30 per cent of the city's tower blocks had been demolished in what he terms 'an orgy' or 'frenzy of demolition', Leslie refers to the loss of history, homes and memories and the scattering of communities across the city as a repeat of the experience of the 1960s.[107] While councillors may 'celebrate the death of high-rise as progress', Leslie asks whether the city is locked into a repetitive cycle of demolition, new-build and reinvention, with 'today's solution becoming tomorrow's problem', as it had last century.[108] Although this seems an unfair comparison to make between mid-twentieth century tower blocks and the high quality houses with gardens to which recently relocated residents have moved and which they appreciate, it may not be so unfair in relation to the re-provision of high-rise dwellings in the city in the twenty-first century, mostly in the private sector.

The return of a second generation of high-rise residential developments in the city has taken three main forms, all in the private sector: waterfront housing along the river Clyde; student housing; and build-to-rent accommodation. Glasgow's waterfront housing, much of it in newly-built multi-storey blocks of between six and over twenty storeys, has been described as an example of 'flagship regeneration', with aims of changing the image of a post-industrial city and being a catalyst for further growth and investment.[109] In this sense, high-rise developments in the twenty-first century play a similar role to those of the mid-twentieth century. However, the Clyde Waterfront developments are also part of an attempt to convert the city to one based on a service sector economy (financial services in the case of the riverside area) and combine this with culture-led renewal wherein residential provision occurs alongside such developments as a media quarter on one side of the river and a museums quarter on the other.[110]

Another departure from the past is that the Glasgow Harbour project is private-sector led and portrayed as 'new build gentrification'. Glasgow City Plan 1, dating from 2002, sought to achieve renewal of a 30 kilometre stretch along the river known as the Clyde Corridor, through new conference and leisure facilities and 'up-market housing designed to attract young professionals working in the new economy'.[111] Although, as in the 1950s, Glasgow's approach is partly driven by a desire to reverse population loss through high-density housing development, retain or attract people to the city, and collect more local tax income, unlike the post-war developments the more recent high rise along the river is aimed at middle-class, affluent households which the city is seen as lacking.[112] The first two phases of Glasgow Harbour, at the heart of the Clyde Corridor, between the city centre and its west end, included approximately 1,500 flats, mostly multi-storey. But rather than attract middle-class families back into the city, early evidence from sales at Glasgow Harbour revealed a lot of purchasing activity by speculators and investors, who would go on to re-sell or, after the financial downturn in 2008, let their properties, thus creating a somewhat different kind of residential area than planned.[113]

The expansion of the city's universities over the past two decades has been the source of further growth in high-rise accommodation for students. By the end of 2017 it was estimated that the city had nearly 18,000 student bedspaces in dedicated developments, nearly 40 per cent owned by universities themselves and the rest in the private sector. Much of this comprises multi-storey flats with a strong focus on attracting increasing numbers of foreign students who can pay relatively high rents for accommodation in buildings with collective amenities such as gymnasiums and shops. A further 6,000 bedspaces for students were reported as planned in spring 2018, bringing the number of dedicated developments to nearly 90.[114] Alongside student flats, there have also more recently been plans for the development of multi-storey build-to-rent housing in central Glasgow located near offices and alongside the river Clyde, marking a new departure for the city in terms of the intended use of high rise.[115]

It would appear therefore as if the future of high-rise housing is being consolidated through private sector development where once it was secured through the social sector. Whether the Grenfell Tower tragedy casts a shadow over this future remains to be seen. Some of the private sector developments in the city stalled for a while due to concerns about combustible cladding, initially estimated as affecting 57 private sector high-rise developments, but later amended to 19, while over 300 social sector tower blocks were identified as lacking sprinkler systems to tackle fires, although GHA reported that none of its towers had combustible cladding.[116] While GHA has confirmed that demand for its remaining high-rise housing is high and sustainable, some other local authorities such as North Ayrshire and North Lanarkshire on the city's boundaries have suggested that they may demolish their tower blocks as future investment in them was not justified and would not bring them up to modern standards.[117] Thus, while the social housing sector seems to have retreated from high-rise housing to a large extent (though by no means entirely), the private sector seems as committed to it as a built form as ever, at least for specific lifestyles and social groups.

A retrospective study of the post-war high-rise experience

It is a paradox that despite the predominantly negative image associated with the first-generation of high-rise flats – that they failed both physically and socially – the city of Glasgow, like other cities in the UK, has embarked on a second-generation of high-rise development in the twenty-first century. This prompts a re-examination of the experience of high-rise flats in the second half of the twentieth century, to understand what it was like for those who moved to, lived in, and grew-up in Glasgow's post-war tower blocks. Such a reconsideration can help to confirm or question the existing myths and conventional wisdoms about high-rise living, but also understand in what ways high rise functioned well or not so well, in order to inform expectations and shape design and management approaches to the second-generation high rise built since the millennium or yet to be constructed.

Our study of Glasgow's post-war high-rise experience is a follow-up to the major early study conducted by the social scientist Pearl Jephcott at the University of Glasgow. The study on 'The social implications of domestic housing in high flats' was undertaken from 1966 to 1969 and aimed to place tenants' 'feelings' centre-stage, as the chief form of data to be employed in assessing the 'social implications' of high flat living. In the words of the authors of the earlier study,

> People and their homes rather than housing in the usual sense of the word are the subject of this study, and in particular the feelings of those who live there as to whether a high flat helps them to improve the quality of their life, that fuller life which most of us would like....[118]

According to the authors, the study was funded because of concerns about the effects of high-rise living on families and young children in particular, and 'the attrition of social life that [tower buildings and high slabs] may be inducing'.[119] The focus was to be on 'social issues, ignoring as far as proved workable those aspects of housing connected with densities, costs, architectural design and aesthetics', and on 'practical matters relating to the day-to-day life of the multi-storey population [rather] than with the longer-distance social implications'.[120] However, practical matters led the research team to focus very much on aspects of the interior and exterior design of the flats, buildings and estates in reporting their findings, especially in relation to families with children and older people (with discussion of drying areas, play facilities, balconies and lifts). The research was also influenced by prior concerns about the height, scale and 'sameness' of high-rise estates built in Britain and Glasgow compared with those built abroad at the time. As the researchers state: 'the point is important because the looks of the immediate environment and the quality of services are probably more important to those who live in a high flat than in a home of traditional type'.[121]

Jephcott, assisted by Hilary Robinson and a wider team of students and market researchers, conducted an ambitious research programme which combined quantitative and qualitative methods. The team aimed to gather a sample of residents' responses from all the high flat developments in the city (numbering 49 developments containing 143 separate blocks).[122] This commenced with an initial 5 per cent sample of 7,732 households in February 1967 followed by the main 5 per cent sample of 14,658 households in July 1968. Almost 1,000 households eventually gave interviews.[123] The responses were gathered in the form of answers to market-research style questionnaires conducted with householders in their own homes. The content of the questionnaires focused on residents' views on the flat, the block and the estate with the emphasis on the material and physical environment. The survey permitted some free-form comment and also elicited opinions on provision for children's play. Researchers also collected information pertaining to social contact as well as data concerning the economic and social profiles of tenants, their prior housing circumstances and rental and utility costs.[124]

In addition to the data collected from tenants, Jephcott amassed an extensive archive of materials relating to high flat living and commissioned a number of separate studies – on lift waiting times, graffiti, mothers and pre-school children, and tenants' associations – carried out by her students. There was only one published outcome from the project, the book *Homes in High Flats,* which presents a summation of the data gathered as well as Jephcott's more discursive analysis of the impact of high-rise living on individuals and families with a particular focus on mothers with young children, the elderly, social contact and the physical environment.[125] The High Flats collection at the University of Glasgow Archive contains all the project data – including all of the 1,000-plus questionnaires – permitting us to follow in Jephcott's footsteps as she came to know Glasgow's high-rise communities.

Ultimately, Jephcott's findings turned out to be more ambiguous than she anticipated. Expectations that the survey results would reinforce the view that high-rise living was unpopular and resulted in social disintegration were dashed as the overwhelming majority of respondents, 91 per cent, indicated that they were 'satisfied' with their new homes. In the context of objective housing conditions in Glasgow, the vastly improved material circumstances of most of those who were rehoused in high flats and the structured questionnaire format employed by the research team, this conclusion based on the question, 'On the whole are you satisfied or not with living here? Yes: No', is hardly surprising.[126] The vast majority were offered little or no choice of housing style upon being rehoused to a high flat. Yet, while Jephcott was a little nonplussed by the high satisfaction score, positing that respondents may just have been expressing delight at living in a 'convenient and attractive home' or were merely mirroring the 'stylish attitude', in *Homes in High Flats* she screened out the 'unreliable' tenants' voices in order to present an interpretation of high-rise living that accorded more closely with her own truth about this form of housing. The questionnaire returns, or at least the quantitative data derived from them, did not provide the clear evidence for isolation and social dislocation that Jephcott anticipated. However, having reviewed the questionnaires more fully, especially taking into account the free comments elicited by the interviewers, it is clear that tenants offered up a wider range of views that could not be contained within the question and answer, yes or no, format, particularly in response to several open questions. The questionnaires thus provide a more subjective and nuanced evidential base for understanding the individual and the social experience of living in a high flat in Glasgow in the 1960s than Jephcott allowed for, and thus we return to them in our follow-up research.

The study archive provides a rich body of material with which to gain access to the high-rise experience as it was lived in the first few years of the experiment. It offers an unparalleled insight into how social tenants from young mothers to elderly singletons, negotiated the move from more traditional housing – mostly tenements – to a modern high flat and how they rationalised their often complex and ambivalent feelings about living on a vertical street. Our own research comprised three elements. First, we undertook a re-analysis of a sample of the High Flats questionnaires, transcribing the responses from all of the surveyed households from four case study estates: Castlemilk, Gorbals, Moss Heights and Wyndford.[127] These contained a series of open questions towards the end on respondents' likes and dislikes about their house, block and scheme (estate), and about how their social life had changed since moving to the high-rise blocks. This verbatim material was not included in the analyses carried out by the original research team which focused on the majority of closed questions in the survey. Second, we examined archive material about high-rise developments in Glasgow, both held within the High Flats study collection and elsewhere. Third, we conducted oral history interviews with people who moved to the high-rise estates, a few as tenants, but most with their parents as children. The earliest interviewee moved to Moss Heights in 1957; the most recent moved to Castlemilk as a child in 1981. Twenty-three participants, the majority of whom had or still lived on our four study estates – men and women with ages ranging from 46 to 90 – were recruited through social media, a study website and through public engagement events on the theme of Multi-Storey Memories. A small number still lived in a high-rise flat but the majority had moved to other forms of housing, both public and owner occupied, though most had remained in Glasgow. The interviews were conducted using life history methodology, with memories of life in the high rise related to other life events and societal developments at the time. Thus our interviews ranged much more widely in content than Jephcott's market-research style questions and facilitated a more in-depth consideration of their experience of high-rise living, both at the time and in retrospect.[128]

We selected four of the estates with high rise that were also included in Jephcott's earlier study – Castlemilk, Gorbals, Moss Heights and Wyndford – and focused on these in our re-analysis, archival research and oral histories. In two of the selected cases, Moss Heights and Wyndford, the high-rise flats still exist today, and in the two other cases they have been partially or completely demolished. Our four case-studies exemplify different kinds of high-rise development.

Castlemilk is one of Glasgow's four peripheral housing schemes and here the high flats were built within an existing inter-war council-housing estate (comprising low rise modern tenements built in the 1950s) to the south of the city, an estate already suffering from isolation and lack of amenity. Nine 20-storey blocks were approved and built by Wimpey between 1960 and 1966 comprising three 20-storey blocks in Dougrie Place which were built in the middle of the estate near the recently constructed shopping centre, a single 20-storey block at Bogany Terrace and five blocks at Mitchelhill situated on a semi-rural, elevated and exposed site a 20-minute walk from shops and schools and housing large numbers of children. While the Dougrie flats are still standing, Bogany was demolished in 1993 and Mitchelhill in 2005. Most of our data relates to Mitchelhill.

The Wyndford estate, by contrast, was situated in the north-west of the city centre on the site of the former military barracks at Maryhill, an established working-class community. The development was conceived on a massive scale, consisting of four 26-storey blocks of 150 dwellings each; five 15-storey blocks; three seven-storey blocks as well as three and four storey courtyard housing, two primary schools, a nursery school and several shops. This was to accommodate around 1,900 families, totalling some 6,000 people. This massive undertaking was built at a frenetic and constant pace between 1961 and 1969, only possible due to the employment of cutting-edge building materials and methods. Built in part by the Corporation's Direct Labour, in part by John Laing Construction Ltd, the pace of construction was enhanced and the costs controlled through extensive use of 'systems building' and 'no fines concrete', a lightweight concrete cast in situ. Within the multi-storey blocks, space was organised so as to inculcate 'communal feeling' amongst tenants; the 26-storey blocks contained six flats to a floor, all connected by a communal balcony intended to re-create the working-class sociability of the tenement 'stairheid'. The Wyndford flats remain standing today.

Moss Heights sited in Cardonald in the south-west of the city, depicted here in Figure 1.3, was the first experiment in the use of high-rise flats for rehousing without resorting to population dispersal outwith the city core. Built between 1950 and 1954, using a reinforced concrete frame structure, the development accommodated 263 dwellings, comprising 219 four-apartment

Figure 1.3 Moss Heights, the first multi-storey flats in Glasgow completed in 1954, designed by Glasgow Corporation's Director of Housing, Ronald Bradbury.

flats in three ten-storey blocks, and 48 three and four apartment flats in two four storey blocks. Moss Heights, unlike most other high flats in the city, was built and promoted as 'modern luxury flats', equipped with 'all modern amenities' and allocated to better-off working class and lower middle-class tenants, many of them families. The location, on a high, north-south facing ridge, also ensured a maximum of daylight consumption, a panoramic view of green south Glasgow and plenty of access to green space for the tenants. Moss Heights is still standing, has been recently refurbished and remains popular today.

Finally, the Gorbals/Hutchesontown estate is probably the most well-known Glasgow neighbourhood, notorious since the nineteenth century for its slums and associated overcrowding, poverty and poor health. It was designated a Comprehensive Development Area in 1957 and prestigious and well-known architects were awarded contracts to build high-rise estates with a 'modern' aesthetic, reflecting contemporary architectural fashion and practice. Hutchesontown 'A' – predominantly low rise housing – was completed in the late 1950s to be followed by Hutchesontown 'B', comprising four 18 storey blocks, designed by Robert Mathew, and Hutchesontown 'C', otherwise known as Queen Elizabeth Square, designed by Sir Basil Spence comprising three high-rise slab blocks. 'D' and 'E' completed the scheme adding six 24-storey blocks and some lower-rise and deck access flats. Our focus was on Spence's Hutchesontown 'C' – 400 individual flats linked by communal balconies in blocks built on stilts, described officially as 'the most complex of all the city's multi-storey blocks' and by an ex-resident as 'like a flying saucer taking you to Mars'.[129] The flats were demolished in 1993.

In the chapters that follow, we concentrate on three key themes pertaining to the experience of post-war high-rise residents. First, in Chapter 2, we focus on high-rise interiors, not merely in a physical, functional and technical manner like the Jephcott team, but rather as spaces of identity and opportunity, thus offering a perspective on high-rise living rarely encountered. Although tower blocks have been described as a means of social control, the high-rise flat also offered a 'modern' space that enabled working-class participation in the post-war consumer boom and design revolution involving domestic goods and home improvements.[130] We explore how occupants adopted design practices within their high-rise flats to adapt the spaces to meet their tastes and needs and create domestic privacy, sometimes for the first time. We show that occupants appreciated and enjoyed their homes, not only for the material comforts they provided but for the opportunity to create a cosy domesticity. In this chapter we also draw attention to the tension between the ability to retreat into the family home and the demands made by the communal requirements of the block.

We show that over time social interactions in the block declined and collective routines became more difficult to maintain as the population of blocks became more fluid. The result was that domestic privacy was all that remained and even that, in some locations, was threatened or transformed partly into isolation and loneliness. The community of the floor or block which had always been built on a fragile reciprocity began to break down in some towers in part because original residents became isolated and new occupants were uninterested in maintaining a residential community.

Chapter 3 looks outside the home to consider what life was like on high-rise estates, focusing on the contrast between an inner city and a peripheral location. Here we consider first residents' responses to estate design (including the provision of amenities) to examine the degree to which the location of the estate and the environment beyond the block affected people's everyday experience, responses that were clearly shaped by different gender roles. We show that despite people's enjoyment of their flat, the 'symbolic violence' of the estate comprising broken and vandalised amenities and unyielding environments, could be detrimental to adults' wellbeing and a barrier to social interaction. We also take a close look at provision for children's play, a recurring issue in disadvantaged areas, and show that while parents' views about play provision mirrored those of social researchers – that designated play facilities were necessary and that high flats were inappropriate for children – children's experiences emphasise adaptability and creativity in the high flats environment.

Many estates earned a poor reputation for vandalism, antisocial behaviour and its range of causes, some of them related to design and maintenance deficiencies on estates, but others to do with social and economic change and the retreat from community. This theme is taken further in Chapter 4 where we consider the question of whether communities on high-rise estates inevitably declined due to design flaws and physical deterioration, or whether the estates were adversely affected by social residualisation and stigmatisation within wider society; in other words, did internal social deterioration have external as well as internal causes. And in the light of these changes, we explore how residents reflect a loss of respectability in the discursive trajectories and narratives they communicate about their estates, and adapt their neighbourly relations in response to social decline. Throughout all three chapters we grapple with the relationship between privacy and sociability, individualism and community, themes which have dominated the social investigation of British society since the 1940s and which continue to have salience in contemporary discussions of the nature of urban society.[131]

The narrative of decline and failure dominates interpretations of high-rise housing in the city but this narrative rests almost entirely upon a perspective that gives greater weight to the form of this kind of housing and to external policy decisions than to the experience of those who lived in the high flats. It is undeniable that by the early 1980s some high-rise estates in the city were beset with problems, from lack of maintenance to anti-social behaviour. Changing occupancy profiles on some estates altered established patterns of behaviour within blocks leaving long term residents feeling anxious about cleanliness, functionality and security. The neighbourliness, friendships and communality that had been built up in the early decades began to dissipate as people moved away. But this is not the whole story.

Few of those who were rehoused to a high flat in this era would have chosen to live in this form of housing notwithstanding the attraction of modernity manifested in in the towers. Glaswegians were just as desirous of a house with a front door as anyone else. But most accommodated themselves to high rise, the comfort and privacy it offered for a time outweighing the disadvantages. This spirit of compromise was evident in people's responses to Jephcott's survey in the 1960s and again in our own oral history interviews. In the chapters that follow we privilege the voices of those who were the pioneers of Glasgow's high-rise experiment to better interpret the long-term history of a housing model that has been so widely denigrated.

Notes

1 Ronald Miller and Joy Tivy (eds), *The Glasgow Region: A General Survey* (T & A Constable, Edinburgh, 1958), p. 4.
2 R. Miller, 'The New Face of Glasgow', *Scottish Geographical Magazine*, vol. 86:1 (1970), p. 5.
3 See the promotional images in, for example, Glasgow Corporation, *Farewell to the Single-End* (City of Glasgow District Council, Glasgow, 1974); A.G. Jury, *Housing Centenary. A Review of Municipal Housing in Glasgow from 1866 to 1966* (Glasgow Corporation Housing Department, Glasgow, 1966).
4 See Miles Glendinning and Stefan Muthesius, *Tower Block: Modern Public Housing in England, Scotland, Wales, and Northern Ireland* (Yale University Press, New Haven, CT, 1994), chapter 32.
5 Michael Pacione, 'Renewal, redevelopment and rehabilitation in Scottish cities 1945–1981', in George Gordon (ed.), *Perspectives of the Scottish City* (Aberdeen University Press, Aberdeen, 1985), pp. 280–305; Andrew Gibb, *Glasgow: The Making of a City* (Croom Helm, London, 1983).
6 Pearl Jephcott with Hilary Robinson, *Homes in High Flats: Some of the Human Problems Involved in Multi-Storey Housing* (Oliver & Boyd, Edinburgh, 1971), p. 4.
7 Scottish Government 'Stock by Tenure 2018': www2.gov.scot/Topics/Statistics/Browse/Housing-Regeneration/HSfS/KeyInfoTables (accessed 26.11.2019). Statistics for England: https://fullfact.org/economy/whats-happening-rented-social-housing-england/ (accessed 26.11.2019).

8 The exception are architectural historians. See Miles Horsey, *Tenements and Towers: Glasgow Working-Class Housing 1890–1990* (RCAHMS, Edinburgh, 1990); Miles Glendinning and Stefan Muthesius, *Towers for the Welfare State: An Architectural History of British Multi-Storey Housing 1945–1970* (Scottish Centre for Conservation Studies, Edinburgh, 2017). See also Alison Ravetz, *Council Housing and Culture: The History of a Social Experiment* (Routledge, London, 2003), p. 104.

9 Notably Michael Young and Peter Willmott, *Family and Kinship in East London* (Penguin, Harmondsworth, 1957); Peter Willmott and Michael Young, *Family and Class in a London Suburb* (Penguin, London, 1960). See Jon Lawrence, *Me, Me, Me! The Search for Community in Post War England* (Cambridge University Press, Cambridge, 2019) for re-analysis of a number of social surveys of this era.

10 Richard Rodger (ed.), *Scottish Housing in the Twentieth Century: Policy and Politics 1885–1985* (Leicester University Press, Leicester, 1989), p. 22.

11 Andrew Gibb, 'Policy and politics in Scottish housing since 1945' in Rodger, *Scottish Housing*, pp. 155–82.

12 The 'Glasgow effect' refers to the greater vulnerability of greater Glasgow's population – owing to historical processes and political decisions – to a range of influences on health including poverty, deindustrialisation and deprivation. For the view that considers housing policy in this mix see Chik Collins and Ian Levitt, 'The modernisation of Scotland and its impact on Glasgow, 1955–1979: unwanted side effects and vulnerabilities', *Scottish Affairs* 25:3 (2016), pp. 294–316.

13 Darren McGarvey, *Poverty Safari. Understanding the Anger of Britain's Underclass* (Luath Press, Edinburgh, 2017), p. 56.

14 Examples include: Lynsey Hanley, *Estates: An Intimate History* (Granta, London, 2012); John Grindrod, *Concretopia: A Journey around the Rebuilding of Postwar Britain* (Old Street, London, 2014); John Boughton, *Municipal Dreams: the Rise and Fall of Council Housing* (Verso, London, 2018); Ben Rogaly and Becky Taylor, *Moving Histories of Class and Community: Identity, Place and Belonging in Contemporary England* (Palgrave, Basingstoke, 2011); Sean Damer, *Scheming: a Social History of Glasgow Council Housing* (Edinburgh University Press, Edinburgh, 2019); Guy Ortolano, *Thatcher's Progress. From Social Democracy to Market Liberalism through an English New Town* (Cambridge University Press, Cambridge, 2019).

15 Glendinning and Muthesius, *Tower Block*; Horsey, *Tenements and Towers.*

16 Hanley, *Estates*, p. 146.

17 Boughton, *Municipal Dreams*; Ravetz, *Council Housing.*

18 Ravetz, *Council Housing*; Patrick Dunleavy, *The Politics of Mass Housing in Britain, 1945–1975: A Study of Corporate Power and Professional Influence in the Welfare State* (Clarendon Press, Oxford, 1981); Gibb, 'Policy and politics'; Coleman, *Utopia on Trial: Vision and Reality in Planned Housing* (Hilary Shipman, London, 1990); Glendinning and Muthesius, *Tower Block.*

19 See, for example, Ade Kearns, Elise Whitley, Phil Mason and Lyndal Bond, '"Living the high life"? Residential, social and psychosocial outcomes for high-rise occupants in a deprived context', *Housing Studies*, 27:1 (2012), pp. 97–126; Robert Gifford, 'The consequences of living in high-rise buildings', *Architectural Science Review* 50:1 (2006), pp. 2–17; Eva van Kempen and Sako Musterd, 'High-rise housing reconsidered: some research and policy

implications', *Housing Studies* 6:2 (1991), pp. 83–95. On Glasgow in particular see the publications and research papers produced by the Go-Well research project at the University of Glasgow which conducted a ten-year project to investigate the impact of investment in housing, regeneration and neighbourhood renewal in Glasgow on the health and wellbeing of individuals, families and communities. www.gowellonline.com (accessed 26.11.2019).

20 Jane Jacobs, *The Death and Life of Great American Cities* (Pimlico, New York: 1961); Coleman, *Utopia on Trial.*
21 Kearns *et al.*, 'Living the high life?', pp. 115–17.
22 'New research identifies high rise as answer to housing crisis', https://labmonline.co.uk/news/uponor-report-high-rise-social-housing-crisis/ (accessed 26.11.2019).
23 The research – 'The social implications of domestic housing in high flats' – funded by the Joseph Rowntree Memorial Trust was led by Pearl Jephcott with the assistance of Hilary Robinson. The project materials are held by University of Glasgow Archives (DC 126).
24 Glasgow City Archives (GCA): DTC/7/12/3: *Housing News*, No 8, vol. 1, June 1947.
25 Martin Taulbut, David Walsh, Gerry McCartney and Charles Collins, *Excess Mortality and Urban Change* (NHS Health Scotland, Glasgow, 2016), Table 2, p. 28.
26 Glendinning and Muthesius, *Tower Block*, p. 156.
27 R. Bruce, First Planning Report to the Highways and Planning Committee of the Corporation of the City of Glasgow, Corporation of the City of Glasgow, Glasgow. *The Bruce Report* (1945).
28 Jephcott, *Homes in High Flats*, p. 14.
29 David Walsh, Gerry McCartney, Charles Collins, Martin Taulbut and G.D. Batty, *History, Politics and Vulnerability: Explaining Excess Mortality in Scotland and Glasgow* (Glasgow Centre for Population Health, Glasgow, 2016), Figure 14, p. 39.
30 A.G. Jury, *Housing Centenary*, p. 61. See also Glasgow Corporation, *City of Glasgow Development Plan: Quinquennial Review 1960* (Glasgow: Glasgow Corporation Architectural and Planning Department), 1960.
31 R. Bruce, First Planning Report.
32 Taulbut *et al.*, *Excess Mortality*, Figure 4, p. 25.
33 Taulbut *et al.*, *Excess Mortality*, Table 2.
34 Richard Turkington, 'Britain: high rise housing as a "doubtful guest"' in R. Turkington, R. van Kempen and F. Wassenberg (eds) *High-Rise Housing in Europe: Current Trends and Future Prospects* (DUP Science, Delft, 2004), pp. 147–64.
35 Glendinning and Muthesius, *Tower Block*, pp. 157–8.
36 Corporation of the City of Glasgow, *Report on the Clearance of Slum Houses, Redevelopment and Overspill* (Glasgow, 1957).
37 Glendinning and Muthesius, *Tower Block*, chapter 20.
38 Jephcott, *Homes in High Flats*, p. 15.
39 Glendinning and Muthesius, *Tower Block*, p. 161.
40 Jephcott, *Homes in High Flats*, p. 18 and Table 3.
41 *Housing Management in Scotland* (1960) cited in Jephcott, *Homes in High Flats*, p. 17.
42 Glendinning and Muthesius, *Tower Block*, p. 170.

43 Historic Environment Scotland Archive (HES): MS2329/STC/37/1. Newspaper cutting from *Scottish Daily Express* (undated, *c*.1962).
44 P.A. Stone, 'The economics of housing and urban development', *Journal of the Royal Statistical Society Series A (General)*, 122:4 (1959), p. 417.
45 Stephen Merrett, *State Housing in Britain* (Routledge and Kegan Paul, London, 1979).
46 Glendinning and Muthesius, *Tower Block*, p. 162.
47 Glasgow City Archives (GCA), Minutes of the Corporation of Glasgow, Housing Committee, 13 January 1954, p. 1392.
48 The *Glasgow Herald*, '"Not Proven" Verdict on 17 Storey Flats', 9 June 1954, p. 7. See also the *Glasgow Herald*, 'Delegation Visit French Flats', 27 February 1954, p. 5 and '"Flats on Stilts" Inspected', 4 March 1954, p. 4.
49 The *Glasgow Herald*, '"Not Proven" Verdict on 17 Storey Flats', 9 June 1954, p. 7.
50 *Scottish Daily Express*, 28 March 1964, p. 9.
51 GCA, SRA TC-1117 (Gibson Files): The *Glasgow Herald* – 22 September and 25 September 1959.
52 GCA, SRA TC-1117 (Gibson Files): undated press cutting, c.1963–4.
53 Figures for England and Wales cited in Merrett, *State Housing*, graph 5.2.
54 Turkington, *High-Rise Housing in Europe*, p. 151.
55 City of Glasgow District Council Housing Department, *Annual Housing Review 1984*, p. 151.
56 Ian Cole and Robert Furbey, *The Eclipse of Council Housing* (Routledge, London, 1994), p. 77.
57 Merrett, *State Housing*, p. 128.
58 Andrew Thomas, *Housing and Urban Renewal* (Allen & Unwin, London, 1986), p. 65.
59 Young and Willmott, *Family and Kinship*; Hilda Jennings, *Societies in the Making: A Study of Development and Redevelopment Within a County Borough* (Routledge, London, 1962).
60 Lionel Needleman, 'The comparative economics of improvement and new building', *Urban Studies*, 6:2 (1969), pp. 196–209; E.M. Sigsworth and R.K. Wilkinson, 'Rebuilding or renovation', *Urban Studies*, 4:2 (1967), pp. 109–21.
61 Ministry of Housing and Local Government *Circular 65/69*.
62 Ministry of Housing and Local Government, *House Condition Survey England and Wales, 1967*.
63 Joan Maizels, *Two to Five in High Flats*: *An Enquiry into Play Provision for Children aged Two to Five Years Living in High Flats* (Housing Centre Trust, London, 1961); S. Saegert, 'Environments and children's mental health: Residential density and low income children', in A. Baum and J.E. Singer (eds), *Handbook of Psychology and Health* (Vol. 2), (Lawrence Erlbaum, Hillsdale, NJ, 1981), pp. 247–71.
64 Jephcott, *Homes in High Flats*, p. 140.
65 See Brown *et al.* 1975.
66 N.C. Moore, 'The personality and mental health of flat dwellers', *British Journal of Psychiatry*, 128:3 (1975), pp. 259–61; D.A. Cook and H.G. Morgan, 'Families in high rise flats', *British Medical Journal*, 284: 6319 (1982), p. 846.
67 City of Glasgow District Council *Annual Housing Review* 1984, p. 151.
68 Jephcott, *Homes in High Flats*, p. 141.

69 Boughton, *Municipal Dreams*, p. 142.
70 Ibid., p. 143.
71 City of Glasgow District Council, *Annual Housing Review 1984*, p. 153.
72 City of Glasgow District Council, *Annual Housing Review 1983*, p. 170.
73 Glasgow City Council, *House Condition Survey* 1985, Vol. 3.
74 City of Glasgow District Council, *Annual Housing Review 1982*, p. 66.
75 Secretary of State Noble at the opening of Hutchesontown 'B' in 1962.
76 Coleman, *Utopia on Trial;* Oscar Newman, *Defensible Space: Crime Prevention through Urban Design* (Collier Books, New York, 1973).
77 Boughton, *Municipal Dreams*, pp. 182–3.
78 Anne Power, *Priority Estates Project 1982: Improving Problem Council Estates* (Department of the Environment, London, 1982).
79 Gavin McCrone, 'Urban renewal: the Scottish experience', *Urban Studies*, 28:6 (1991), pp. 919–38.
80 Michael Harloe, 'The green paper on housing policy' in M. Brown and S. Baldwin (eds) *The Year Book of Social Policy in Britain 1977* (Routledge & Kegan Paul, London, 1978), pp. 3–21.
81 Peter Malpass and Alan Murie, *Housing Policy and Practice* (Macmillan, London, 1982).
82 Ray Forrest and Alan Murie, 'Residualization and council housing: aspects of the changing social relations of housing tenure', *Journal of Social Policy*, 12:4 (1983), pp. 453–68; Jen Pearce and Jim Vine, 'Quantifying residualisation: the changing nature of social housing in the UK', *Journal of Housing and the Built Environment*, 29 (2014), pp. 657–75.
83 Michael Harloe, *The People's Home: Social Rented Housing in Europe and America* (Blackwell, Oxford, 1995), p. 290.
84 Boughton, *Municipal Dreams*, p. 143.
85 Forrest and Murie, 'Residualization'.
86 City of Glasgow District Council, *Annual Housing Review 1982*, Table 2.6.
87 City of Glasgow District Council, *Annual Housing Review 1982*, Table 2.1 and *Glasgow House Condition Survey 1985*, Table 4.5.
88 City of Glasgow District Council, *Annual Housing Review* 1984, Table 3.25.
89 David Clapham and Keith Kintrea, 'Rationing, choice and constraint: the allocation of public housing in Glasgow', *Journal of Social Policy* 15:1 (1986), pp. 51–67.
90 Duncan Maclennan, *Housing in Scotland 1977–87* (Centre for Housing Research, Glasgow, 1980), p. 33.
91 Maclennan, *Housing in Scotland*, p. 33.
92 Maclennan, *Housing in Scotland*, p. 37.
93 Duncan Maclennan and Andrew Gibb, *Glasgow: No Mean City to Miles Better*, Discussion Paper 18. (Centre for Housing Research, Glasgow, 1988), Table 6.
94 Boughton, *Municipal Dreams*, pp. 143–4.
95 Boughton, *Municipal Dreams*, p. 162.
96 Boughton, *Municipal Dreams*, p. 163.
97 City of Glasgow District Council, *Annual Housing Review 1982*, p. 59.
98 Kenneth Gibb 'Transferring Glasgow's council housing: financial, urban and housing policy implications', *European Journal of Housing Policy* 3:1 (2003), pp. 89–114.
99 City of Glasgow District Council, *30-Year Business Plan* (2004), p. 41.

100   Ibid.
101   City of Glasgow District Council, *30-Year Business Plan* (2004), p. 42.
102   City of Glasgow District Council, *Asset Management Position Statement* (2006), p. 24.
103   Ibid., p. 23.
104   For recent research see Kearns *et al.*, 'Living the high life?'. And on responses to demolition, M. McLaughlin, 'Glasgow will regret pulling down "eyesore" high-rises', *The Scotsman*, 5 May 2018.
105   www.bruteurope2018.eu/ (accessed 08.05.2019).
106   C. Leslie, 'Disappearing Glasgow: documenting the demolition of a city's troubled past', *Guardian*, 22 April 2015.
107   www.disappearing-glasgow.com/portfolio/introduction/ (accessed 08.05.2019).
108   Ibid.
109   Brian Doucet, *Rich Cities with Poor People. Waterfront Regeneration in the Netherlands and Scotland* (Netherlands Geographical Studies 391, Utrecht, 2016).
110   Michael Pacione, 'The view from the tower: geographies of urban transformation in Glasgow', *Scottish Geographical Journal*, 125:2 (2009), pp. 127–81.
111   John Jackson, 'Neo-liberal or third-way? What planners from Glasgow, Melbourne and Toronto say', *Urban Policy and Research*, 27:4 (2009), pp. 397–417.
112   Brian Doucet, R. van Kempen, and J. van Weesep, '"We're a rich city with poor people": municipal strategies of new-build gentrification in Rotterdam and Glasgow', *Environment and Planning A*, 43 (2011), pp. 1438–54.
113   'Developers sue homebuyers over luxury flats', *The Scotsman*, 12 December 2004.
114   https://athousandflowers.net 'Revealed: 6,000 new private student flats in Glasgow pipeline' (accessed 08.05.2019).
115   www.constructionenquirer.com 'Build-to-rent tower advance reaches Glasgow' (accessed 08.05.2019).
116   K. Bussey, '19 Glasgow tower blocks have Grenfell-style cladding' (2017) www.scotsman.com (accessed 08.05.2019).
117   J. McIvor, 'All council high-rise flats in North Lanarkshire "could come down"', BBC Scotland, 2017, www.bbc.co.uk/news/uk-scotland-glasgow-west-42418148 (accessed 27.12.2019).
118   Jephcott, *Homes in High Flats*, p. 1.
119   Jephcott, *Homes in High Flats*, p. 2.
120   Ibid.
121   Jephcott, *Homes in High Flats*, p. 5.
122   Jephcott, *Homes in High Flats*, p. 21. The project commenced with a pilot study conducted in Clydebank, west of Glasgow.
123   Jephcott, *Homes in High Flats*, p. 27.
124   UGA, DC 127 (High Flats Study).
125   Jephcott, *Homes in High Flats*.
126   Barry Hazley, Valerie Wright, Ade Kearns, Lynn Abrams, '"People and their homes rather than housing in the usual sense"? Locating the tenant's voice in Homes in High Flats'. *Women's History Review*, 28:5 (2019), pp. 728–45.
127   We identified and transcribed all of the questionnaires collected for residents on our four case study estates: Castlemilk, Gorbals, Moss Heights and Wyndford. Each archive box in the collection UGA DC 127/1/1-10/1 contains

a mixture of questionnaires from different estates. The original questionnaires contain identifying information of respondents. In order to adhere to confidentiality requirements, references to questionnaire material have been anonymised, respondents given pseudonyms in the text and specific box numbers have been removed.

128　www.facebook.com/multistoreymemoriesGlasgow/ All interviewees are identified by their real names unless stated otherwise. When transcriptions reproduced spoken dialect we have retained it here.

129　Grindrod, *Concretopia,* p. 156 and p. 165.

130　Boughton, *Municipal Dreams,* p. 179; Judith Attfield, *Bringing Modernity Home. Writings on Popular Design and Material Culture* (Manchester University Press, Manchester, 2007), especially chapter 10.

131　For the most recent iteration of this debate see Lawrence, *Me, Me, Me.*

2 Inside

Making homes – privacy and communality

It is easy to forget that the often brutal exterior of the high-rise block contained scores of flats containing singletons and families who created individual homes with limited resources and the application of creativity. Few studies of high-rise housing venture across the threshold and enter the flat; instead they focus on policy and planning decisions and architectural design.[1] Even Jephcott, who was interested in the everyday experience of residents and whose research team met all their interviewees in their own homes, offered few observations about the inside of the flat.[2] One result is that analysis of this form of housing becomes less about homes and the people who live in them and more about large scale economic and social forces and the architects and officials who designed and planned the new estates.[3] This chapter considers how high-rise occupants became home makers and how they created domestic privacy within high-density housing. It describes the opportunities the flats offered for creativity and the expression of personal taste as well as how people adjusted to living high. By listening to residents' views about everyday decisions and home-making practices expressed in market-research style encounters in the 1960s and some 50 years later in our own oral history interviews, we offer a new narrative of high-rise living which privileges people's emotional and material investment in their homes and goes some way to countering the dominant view, that high-rise housing inevitably produced alienation and social breakdown.[4]

The high-rise flats were a blank canvas in terms of layout and interior design. The individual flats were designed to facilitate private family life. Unlike many sub-standard tenemental flats, where occupants shared spaces and facilities, high-rise flats were more self-contained, insulating each household to a large degree from neighbours. Each block, on the other hand, incorporated shared spaces and facilities which required a modicum of common standards and commitment to cooperation, setting up a tension between the privacy that so many were promised or craved and the communality that was necessary for a functioning community within the block. In what follows we focus first on the flat as a space which enabled residents to express their identity through home décor and their use of the often novel amenities such as balconies and underfloor heating. Many new residents had moved from squalid, overcrowded accommodation in which rooms had multiple functions and considered modern amenities such as hot water and a fixed bath to be luxuries. Through consumption of household goods, use of space, decoration and DIY, we see how the high flats could enable the enjoyment of home life and offer residents the domestic privacy many desired contrasting with the 'enforced sociability' and 'inescapable togetherness' of the tenement.[5] Second, we argue that the creation of a private family life inside the flat existed in tension with the requirements for co-operation and communality within the block. We show that while privacy was highly valued, many desired some level of social interaction with their neighbours and were ready to participate in collective tasks. However, design and maintenance failures and changes in the high flats' population over time ultimately caused many people to privilege privacy over community with the flat becoming a refuge rather than a symbol of social progress.

Modern family homes

In 1961 a promotional film made by Glasgow Corporation proclaimed the benefits of high flats for family life, with particular focus on the functionality and modernity of the new homes. Inside, the flats were presented as the nuclear family's dream: a kitchen with modern conveniences, a living room with space for the family to relax together, separate bedrooms for adults and children, and a balcony – or veranda as it is called in Glasgow – offering mothers a view of their children playing beneath the block. The film featured Moss Heights, the first high-rise development completed in the city in 1954, and the commentary amplified the health and psychological benefits for families of the new housing.

> In this house, with all its modern amenities, the mother can care for her bairns as she has always wanted to. She is no longer haunted by the fear that they have wandered away to some traffic-filled streets or that they are breathing germs of disease in some refuse filled back court. When they come into this house from play she has hot water on tap to wash away the healthy dirt they have collected. Now there is room to live, no longer with all their possessions cluttered together in one apartment. Later the children will go to bed, in their own rooms.[6]

The high flats offered a new template for living. They were designed to be modern, not just in terms of the design of the blocks but also in respect of modern conveniences such as private WCs, hot water, central heating and rubbish chutes, as well as the layout and size of flats and the interior fixtures and fittings. Unlike the overcrowded tenement apartments where many families lived in one or two rooms with sanitary facilities on the shared landing, the new flats had separate rooms designated for cooking, bathing, living and sleeping. These were modern homes designed to be easy to maintain and clean with much use of new products such as Formica and plastics in contrast with the hard to clean and dark wooden fixtures and fittings that were the norm in tenement flats. Indeed, in architect-designed blocks (albeit these were in the minority) the appearance and design of the interior was as important as the build and exterior appearance. The use of new materials and new technology was directly linked to improvements in the quality of home life and more especially for the working-class wife and mother. And despite ample evidence that people preferred, if given a choice, to live in human-proportioned houses on the ground, high-rise flats were proclaimed as offering a planned environment with 'room to breathe' as well as the interior space conducive to a family-centred, modern style of living and participation in consumer culture.[7]

In 1961 the Parker Morris Report, *Homes for Today and Tomorrow,* a response to the new demands of the more affluent home-centred society, commented that:

> an increasing proportion of people are coming to expect their home to do more than fulfil the basic requirements. It must be something of which they can be proud; and in which they must be able to express the fullness of their lives.[8]

This recognition that a house or flat was more than bricks and mortar was acknowledged by Sir Basil Spence, architect of the Queen Elizabeth Square development in the Gorbals, albeit in condescending fashion which cast aspersions on the design choices of working-class occupants of his flats. In 1965 and shortly after the official opening, he acknowledged the independence of 'the tough Scottish Clydesiders' who 'do not accept my colour schemes for the interiors'.

> As soon as they take over the flat, they blitz it in their own way making it cosy, personal and awful taste – to our view – but it has a virile robustness which cannot be denied and in a big plan like this to make each one personal is, in itself, a great virtue.... A glance at the photographs will reveal the diversity of curtain patterns. Believe me, this is only a prelude to the violence of the wallpaper designs that they have.[9]

Figure 2.1 Family in the living room of their fifteenth floor flat in Bogany Terrace, Castlemilk. Jephcott noted 'these children get out very little'.

The image of cosy, colourful flats reflecting their inhabitants' desires for an interior décor that chimed with their own taste, as Figure 2.1 illustrates, contrasts with the image of Glasgow's high flats plagued by damp, lacking sunlight and unfit for human habitation and simultaneously offers a very different perspective to de-personalised representations of high rise as mass housing designed as containers of people.[10] Although Spence's Queen Elizabeth Square incorporated many of the worst features of post-war, brutalist high-rise housing design (vast slabs of grey concrete, windy undercrofts, open expanses and absence of human scale) and eventually succumbed to the ravages of Glasgow's wet weather and maintenance fail-ures, for new tenants in the 1960s these flats offered the opportunity to give rein to their creative instincts. Rather than experiencing alienation, people appropriated the space inside the flats, engaging with modern design to create homes that met their emotional and material needs.[11] Such was many people's desperation for new homes, the desire for decent accommodation trumped any design preferences. The only element of choice offered to prospective tenants was their preference for height. 'Get on with the high flats, never mind the gardens. Homes are what the people want' was one woman's plea to the council.[12] But once they had moved in, while appreciating the provision of facilities such as hot water and electric heating, people expressed strong views on the pros and cons of the design features of their new flats.

We start from the assumption that design is an 'everyday practice of modernity' accessible to everyone, incorporating consumption and display of goods and the creative adaptation and use of space.[13] In the next section we discuss how the residents of high rise, especially those who moved in when flats were new, initially negotiated the use of space in the multi-storeys and how they fashioned individual homes out of identical flats, demonstrating an engagement with and enjoyment of the home as a space for the expression of taste and identity. In the final section we step outside the flat into the shared spaces of the floor and block – the corridors, landings, stairs and lifts and consider how the requirements for common standards and cooperation in the block, far from facilitating neighbourly relations in fact caused dissatisfaction and anxiety from the very start and ultimately instigated a retreat into the privacy or refuge of the flat.

Modern interiors

The modernity of the high flats was most clearly expressed in terms of the design and build features (for instance steel frames, concrete slabs), the internal layout (no parlours, small kitchenettes, interior bathrooms) and the functional and in some cases advanced fixtures and fittings such as refuse chutes and underfloor heating.[14] Tenants were left in no doubt that they were the beneficiaries of homes designed and built with up-to-date improvements and appliances. 'Your new house can truly be called **Modern**, in every sense of the term' stated Glasgow Corporation's 'Notes for the Guidance of Tenants'.

> The wasteful coal fire with its attendant dirt and smoke nuisances, as a source of space heating and hot water supply, has been eliminated and replaced with a modern heating system, operated by Electricity or Gas supply, designed to give continuous warmth throughout your house and to provide a constant and adequate supply of hot water 24-hours per day, at a very economical cost has been embodied in the design and construction.[15]

Modern aesthetics also pervaded the interior of the blocks. The high flats were perceived by their advocates as functional and were designed to incorporate aspects such as lightness and airiness though when Scottish Office civil servants voiced concerns to Glasgow's Housing Department about site layout and especially the potential for some flats to receive limited sunlight owing to their proximity to other high blocks, their concerns were brushed aside.[16] Architects advocated 'simplicity' by the use of large windows and light colour schemes.[17] In the case of Spence's design for Queen Elizabeth Square, the architect himself prescribed the interior colours, rejecting lime green and light blue: 'I feel the colour is too ice cold for corridors which may be low in temperature during the dank days of a Gorbals winter'. He suggested yellow with white ceilings – which 'should remain clean for a long time as they are out of reach', and darker colours for areas that might get marked such as behind the gas fire in the living room.[18] In turn these modern design values were informed by more fundamental assumptions around the health and moral effects of certain design forms. So light, bright, and clean-lined flats were seen to be conducive to improved health outcomes for tenants –and new materials, easy-to-clean surfaces and advanced amenities were expected in Spence's words, 'to make life easier for mothers and housewives'.[19]

Tenants' initial responses to the new homes were largely positive as Jephcott discovered in her survey, somewhat to her surprise. Compared with the often dingy, overcrowded, noisy and poorly appointed tenement accommodation many had left, the high flats were praised for being light, airy, warm and well equipped. Material attractions were still high on tenants' agendas when they were questioned in the late 1960s.[20] 'I love my house. I just love everything in it. The surroundings are lovely and the central heating is marvellous' reported Castlemilk resident Mrs Mitchell.[21] 'I like it – no dislikes. I like the central heating (underfloor) plus the kitchenette worktops and I like the layout of the kitchenette' enthused another female resident of that estate.[22] People were just relieved to be rehoused, summed up by this new resident who was offered a new flat after six years on the housing list: 'The fact that I've never had a house before – I'm grateful for anything'.[23]

In recollections some 50 years on, people still recalled that initial excitement of moving from old fashioned and substandard rented accommodation to a modern home in a high-rise block in terms of function and material comfort rather than status or taste. Leslie Welch, who moved as a child with his parents to a flat in the Moss Heights development, compared the family's former tenement flat with their new home:

> the flat in Renfrew, I remember it being a pretty Victorian, pretty damp, pretty dark, pretty – hot baths, baths, you know, in galvanised tubs that had to be heated up, kettle by kettle. So we were keen to

emerge from that, er, situation. And you know, the opportunity at the Moss Heights came up. Which at the time was a kind of flagship project and not what I would call the norm.[24]

He went on to describe the new flat in more detail:

Well, it was new, it was, you know, modern facilities, it was a completely different form of housing. Well okay with hindsight it's easier to realise what these things were, but it was kind of – there was a degree of pioneering about it. It was the predecessor of many similar schemes, but I think Moss Heights was one of the better examples. Of high-rise living.… Because the way it was planned and designed, was much- it ended up being a very comfortable environment. It had district heating on tap from a central boiler house, large airy rooms, the main living-dining area was kind of open plan and had a balcony which faced south, large windows as opposed to small windows, they were very light and airy, fantastic views, obviously, over Glasgow in both directions, you know, to the surrounding hills, you know, it had all the facilities that we didn't have in the place in Renfrew, in terms of toilet facilities, refuse facilities, drying room, you know, a proper kitchen. But I think one of the biggest benefits was constant running hot water and central heating, you know. It was a new experience, at the time.[25]

Mr Welch, who became an architect, might be expected to look back on his high-rise experience through the lens of his subsequent career. For him, the flat's modernity was manifested in facilities and design but in fact these aspects of the new flats were also recalled by most other interviewees. According to Isabelle who moved to the Mitchelhill flats in Castlemilk as a child in 1964, 'that was the main draw – was the modernity, modernity of it, you know, this high flat'. She elaborated:

Dad had decided this is where we were going, he thought because this was wondrous because you had … the main thing being you didn't have to get up in the mornings and start making a fire anymore, you know, and chipping ice off the windows. These had underfloor heating and you know, there was all mod cons, you know.[26]

John and Carol left 'a building that was almost falling down, it had an outside toilet, cold water by the way … just cold water' and moved to a 'brand new high flat with underfloor heating and a wall fire'.[27] Similarly Brian, who took up residency in the new high flats in the Gorbals in the 1960s recalled:

So we moved tae the flats, so yer first experience ae the flats would huv been 'Oh this is absolutely superb!' It was like moving into the penthouse eh, everything new, lots more room, heating, eh all that sort of thing [laughs].[28]

However, not everyone was so 'satisfied'.[29] While Jephcott's survey revealed broad contentment, it also revealed considerable criticism of the workmanship and, in some blocks, design of the internal flat layout indicating that desperation for a new home did not blind new social tenants to the drawbacks. Causes for complaint included interior bathrooms with no exterior window opening, balconies with rails too low to allow children out or too high for someone sitting down to see over, as Figure 2.2 illustrates, and underfloor heating that did not extend to all rooms and too expensive to turn on. Lorraine recalled her mother only used the underfloor heating in one room:

Oh aye it wis, it wis a treat, but ah know in the winter obviously they must have, 'cause other than that ye were just the bars. An' yet ah

Figure 2.2 Resident of the Wyndford development and the view she cannot see from her chair owing to the height of the wall of the veranda.

don't remember the livin room an' that, ah don't remember sittin bein cold or anything in there, but in yer room aye, ye wur, ye wur freeezin, ye were definitely freezin in yer room.[30]

In her analysis of interior design and taste in another housing context, the post-war new town, Judy Attfield identified conflicts between architects' visions of good design and residents' implementation of popular taste. New town houses' open plan design was often subverted by residents who inserted dividers to create separate living spaces and attempts to design open, airy houses were countered by net and drape curtains and heavy furniture instead of the uncluttered feel that had been envisaged.[31] The home in this period was the site of tensions between the tenets of modernism on the one hand and consumer reaction on the other whereby residents strived to create personal refuges from the outside world, softening sharp modern surfaces and introducing home furnishings and knick-knacks, ornaments and things that personalised the space.[32] This was in part a reaction to wartime and post-war austerity, the end of rationing and the availability of better quality furniture of variable designs replacing utility furniture. Just as in the new town, Glasgow high-rise residents also soon put their own stamp on the modern flats, in the process subverting the intentions of the architect through creativity and necessity.

Space and adaptation

Residents endeavoured to create cosy, liveable spaces that suited families' everyday lifestyles. Decoration was part of the process but just as important was adaptation of the space within the flat to suit family needs. The flats were designed and often marketed as ideal for the nuclear, privatised family, predicated on a gendered division of labour and the shift of family leisure to the home. Yet the families who took up residence in Glasgow's high flats in the first few years came in all shapes and sizes, from singletons to multi-generational households, from families with children to retired couples and dual earners. In Jephcott's sample, 44 per cent of households consisted of adults aged 16 to 65, 27 per cent contained at least one child under 15 and 14 per cent contained elderly adults over 60.[33] In the post-war context all types of family were deemed to deserve a self-contained residence and the high flats contained a range of sizes from the smallest 'studio' designed for singletons (consisting of a tiny 'working kitchen', interior bathroom and a living room with recessed bed space – not unlike the reviled tenement single-end) to three-bedroomed split-level flats for larger families. The rooms were often not as large, and certainly not as tall, as the traditional tenement apartments and the organisation of space – a number of clearly defined functional rooms rather than larger spaces that would have been adapted for a variety of uses from eating to sleeping – meant that in a high flat there were perhaps fewer opportunities for residents to make changes through their domestic behaviour.[34] Reconfiguring the internal space of the flats, either by repurposing rooms (though in many blocks there was no heating in the bedrooms, limiting their use for other purposes) or by erecting dividing walls or other DIY features, was challenging, and rules about the changes tenants were permitted to make varied from block to block. Knocking down walls was not an option in a high flat.[35]

At Moss Heights many complained about the small size of the kitchenette (designed to make housework more efficient and to separate the kitchen from other living spaces) which was not large enough for a family to eat in. 'When these flats were put up they were supposed to have luxury kitchenettes but they are anything but that. I wish a woman had helped to plan these' was one woman's response.[36] Mrs Thallon who has lived most of her adult life in Moss Heights, a woman who valued the whole family sitting down to a meal together around the table, also remarked on the small kitchenette before it was renovated by the housing association: 'but before, ah mean it wis just a wee tiny kitchenette you could never have had a family tae sit down in it ye know, you couldnae, that wis how we just got the table an' chairs up there you know'.[37] Families who had been used to the larger size of rooms in tenements where it might have been usual to have had a dining table in the kitchen-come-living room, now had to find space for this essential piece of furniture in the new layout of the high flat. Mrs Brown who also grew up in Moss Heights recalled the table in the living room: 'It had a space for a dining table, so obviously we ate there and you had your, just your three piece suite.'[38]

However, one feature of a number of blocks did lend itself to a variety of uses. The private balcony, or veranda, was a feature inspired by highrise developments in warmer climes and was intended to create extra private or semi-private space and to improve the outlook.[39] Some verandas were recessed so they aligned with the vertical contours of the block but others protruded from the facade rather alarmingly. Some were private; others were shared or divided from the neighbours by a low wall or fencing. Some were sun traps and others constantly in shade depending on the building's orientation and its proximity to other high-rise blocks. Some verandas appeared to be positively dangerous with low walls or railings meaning that children could never be allowed out onto them, whilst others functioned as play pens. When the wind blew, standing on the veranda could be terrifying or exhilarating. Those in the Gorbals Queen Elizabeth Square development were huge, serving four flats. They were envisaged by the architect as hanging gardens and were certainly big enough for small children to ride a bike.[40] Arguably though, the veranda was a feature which, in colder climates like Scotland, offered few obvious benefits to residents especially when local regulations were imposed to prevent its use for drying washing or other activities that would otherwise have taken place in a yard or garden (keeping pets for instance). Verandas were an architectural affectation included with little attention to local conditions and traditions and it is notable that when old blocks have been refurbished in recent years, verandas have been closed in to create interior and more usable spaces.

Most Glasgow tenants would not have been familiar with a veranda so the uses to which this novel space were put were often not those envisaged by the architects and sometimes contrary to the council's tenant regulations. Some did use it primarily as leisure space. One Gorbals' resident reported liking her veranda as it was 'a) convenient for clothes drying b) view and to sit on c) a possible place in which to escape world and neighbours'.[41] Mrs Williamson who lived in the Wyndford estate and was one of the few who had a veranda on her previous property, recalled how this feature was a real attraction for her when she moved there around 1970:

> The thing that I loved most about when I went in, there was a veranda. Well, I was brought up with a veranda, so I was used to a veranda. So that was everything to me: 'Oh, I've got a veranda. I can go oot there and sit and what not'. And to this day, I still use my veranda.... Then we both worked during the day so at night time, it's a nice night we would just sit out there and our meal and what no'. I think there's many a night I sat there to ten, eleven o'clock at night, depending on the weather. Depending on the weather.[42]

Similarly in Castlemilk, Tricia, who moved there with her parents in 1966, was one of few who recalled the veranda being used for its original purpose, as an access to fresh air and sunshine.

> An' ah remember the first summer we went there must have been quite a good summer because we originally bought sun loungers an' they were out there. Mah mother was actually tanned. They, they were west facing in the veranda so they, the sun round about two o'clock an' then that was it the whole night.... They would sit out there, and at the weekend they would be lying out there as if they were in Monte Carlo, wae Frank Sinatra on the radiogram an' father had got a Soda Stream out ae the Kensitas Coupons 'cause he smoked, an' was very enamoured by that [laughs].... He'd have his Soda, whisky an' Soda,

an' ah think they thought, ye know, it wis like, an' any time ah hear Frank Sinatra ah think ae father clinking wae his ice on the veranda. They thought they'd, thought they'd died an' gone to heaven, so.[43]

In the absence of access to other private or semi-private open space the veranda came to substitute for the tenement back court or yard. The storage of items that could not be found space for in the flat (toys, bicycles), small children's play, keeping pets (birds and small animals such as rabbits) and growing vegetables and flowers in containers were all mentioned. 'I keep my plants on it. I grow my geraniums and I have a lovely display in the summer' reported a male resident of Castlemilk.[44] Paul, whose family moved to the Hutchesontown 'B' scheme in 1967, used the large veranda as a play area but he recalled a wide variety of other uses though sunbathing was not one of them:

That's where people got really creative sometimes.... I think some people used it as an extension to their house ... I remember in Floor 4, they had actually built a sort of like porch to their veranda door onto their veranda.... A lot of people used the verandas as a fridge – so they would have their meats and stuff out there ... the veranda was not, even in the summer, a warm place. It was a cold place. As much as people tried to grow plants and all of that it just didn't work ... I can remember the astro turf back in the day. I think that's where the rise in the plastic planting really took off and that's what people did. They gave up trying to grow stuff. The bottom floor I remember, Floor 1 – Floor 2, was quite successful at that because ... it was south facing, they were always getting that heat because directly opposite the flats they had the lower level roof of the arcade.... So the front of the flats there was a heat trap you know, that was nice. Ground floor you were getting Benidorm sixth floor you were getting Barlinnie – quite different in temperature.[45]

The most obvious functional use of the veranda was for drying laundry but many blocks had rules against this for aesthetic reasons. Mrs Brown recalled how the veranda on her Moss Heights flat was:

a great thing because it meant the ... the living room was very airy because you could open, open the door and ... just on a nice summer's day if you had that to open and had the window open, it, it was like being outside, it was, it was quite pleasant.

But she continued: 'I don't remember people hanging washing out on the balconies, it might have been the rule was you weren't to hang washing out.'[46]

For flats that were so often lauded as ideal for the housewife, the absence of drying facilities either in or outside the blocks appears a cruel omission by architects who had little understanding of the mechanics of doing the weekly wash. The privatisation of household tasks isolated women without giving them the necessary tools for the job. Communal laundry facilities were provided in some blocks though this was a throw-back to the tradition of the 'steamie', the communal wash house, and was increasingly rejected by those who could afford their own washing-machine. Drying the washing was, in the absence of drying greens and before the provision of tumble dryers in the blocks, a perennial problem though those lucky enough to have underfloor heating (and who could afford to use it) report spreading their laundry out on the floors to dry and in one case press under the rugs.[47] Isabelle recalled her mother doing just this:

> ... they had put an electric fireplace in, we didn't have fires obviously, so they put a fireplace in, it had an electric fire in it and they had a big rug sitting, just so that it looked like the rooms you were used to that had a fire as a focal point, you know, and my mum used to ... when she washed the clothes if it was like trousers or jeans, she used to lift the rug and put brown paper down and lay the clothes and put the rug back down, because the heat ... well, it would press them! The heat from the underfloor heating! (Laughter) and the weight of the rug would press the clothes so you didn't need to press them! How she thought of that I don't know.[48]

Residents were loath to use drying cupboards, which were coin operated, because of the expense and communal drying areas – often on the top floor of the block – were regarded as dangerous, difficult to access (the lift in the Mitchelhill blocks at Castlemilk only went to the nineteenth floor, the drying area was on the twentieth) and vulnerable to theft. Tricia recalled the trials of her mother as she tried to get the washing dry on the ground floor of her block:

> An' I only remember my mother hauling both of us and the basket down the lift, going in an' it wis always dark under there, no light or anything, and the wind, created a kind of wind tunnel idea. And so you would be like blowin away [laughs] under. An' mah mum put up the washin and then like she couldnae, she didnae want to leave it because it would be stolen. So we stayed and watched it for a while an' she went, right back down, we all went back upstairs.[49]

Figure 2.3 Hutchesontown 'C' (Queen Elizabeth Square) in the Gorbals. Note the washing drying on the large veranda.

Mothers of babies were especially inconvenienced: 'there is no drying facilities at all in this block for washing' commented a 29-year-old woman with two young children to Jephcott's survey. 'For the nappies we need fresh air but there are no drying areas.'[50] Women who had been used to hanging their washing out on drying greens or even in tenement back courts missed this practice. As a result, many people did use their veranda for hanging out washing, as Figure 2.3 illustrates, although this sometimes aroused the ire of neighbours. As one 57-year-old woman living in Castlemilk said: 'I think its defacing the block when you get folk hanging out the washing on their verandas.'[51] 'It's like a slum here – everywhere you go in Castlemilk there's washing out on all the verandahs. It's terrible' said another, a response that indicated this woman's sense that she had moved up in the world by moving to a high flat and highlights the potential and actual tensions over norms of behaviour.[52] However, Tricia's mother discovered a way of using the veranda for drying her laundry in contravention of the rules and concealed from the view of those who disapproved:

she would have her window on a latch an' she'd put the rope though the window on the latch in the kitchen and then pulled it oot so she pulled it one, two, three, four, fi-, like six stretches using the window, so like one in one out, one in one out, she kept it kind of hangin low so that you didn't see it. But the great thing about that meant that she could still put washin out there in the rain, as long as she kept it back because the balconies eased up into the building an' were protected. And so when she found that, that was her, she just, somebody told her that no tae mention tae anybody that this wis whit to do because it was against the rules. So she did that an' then there was a pulley in the kitchen, so they came in from there an' went up on the pulley. So mah mother had washins oot as many days as she could.[53]

The other main use of the veranda was as a play space for young children in the absence of safe alternatives within a parent's visual field (discussed further in Chapter 3) and contrary to architects' visions who thought the spaces between and sometimes under blocks were ideal for play. The veranda, if sufficiently large and safe, offered fresh air for the children and some relief for parents. Mrs Bradley in Castlemilk admitted she would have preferred 'a back and front door type house' but:

the wee boy has been getting out to play since last year, so that he's not kept in. The verandah's a good thing especially if you've got babies – I could never have mine out before I came here, and if I had another, it could be out on the verandah all day.[54]

The mother of four children including a seven-month old baby living on the Hutchesontown 'B' estate in the Gorbals where the verandas were the size of a room reported that the '2 verandahs are good for putting the baby out on' though the lack of privacy and control over this outside space caused her stress.

Would like my house much better if you could just take it and put it somewhere else. I am sorry I have come to the multi-storey flats. I find them no use with children. No division on the verandahs and children run from one end to the other.[55]

Others were scared their children would come to harm: 'The only thing if the verandah had railings or glass to see through the wee one wouldn't attempt to climb it, but I'm really scared about it.'[56] These communal verandas were not universally popular once more emphasising the desire of residents for privacy.

The reason the veranda occasioned so much comment was that it was often regarded as a wasted space. It was often unsafe, cold and unsuitable for the uses to which exterior spaces might be usefully put. The result of the mismatch between the design of high flats and residents' needs was that residents invested their own values in their homes by contravening rules, using spaces and amenities in ways unimagined by the designers and, as we shall see in the next section, applying their own taste to home décor.

Consumption, décor and taste

For many working-class people in Glasgow, the ability to use the home to express their identity could only happen once they were settled and content in a house or flat which contained all basic services and when they had sufficient disposable income or access to credit to impose their own taste and desires. The 'Homes in High Flats' research did not explicitly seek out people's views on home aesthetics and issues of respectability and distinction. Jephcott was more interested in how people interacted with the buildings and each other than in how they furnished and decorated their homes. However, showing an interest in interior design – for comfort or aesthetics – is indicative of home-making and positive identification with the space. In our oral history interviews we attempted to glean information about how flats were made into homes by asking about discretionary decoration and furnishing. Some scholars have argued that it is primarily through the consumption of material goods that working-class houses become homes in this period, a trend influenced by the rise of mass retail, the availability of cheap, mass-produced consumer goods after the war and of hire purchase and credit schemes and the identification of the home as the primary leisure sphere for all the family.[57] However, few of our oral history respondents spoke at length about interior decoration and home making through consumption. It is likely that financial constraints go some way to explaining this. For many residents the move to a brand new home with all mod cons came at a high price. In many cases, rents doubled or even quadrupled. Whereas 61 per cent of households in Jephcott's study had paid rent and rates of under £4 a month in their previous homes, in the high flats 84 per cent paid between £6 and £10 and more than half reported utility costs as the same or more expensive.[58]

The few surviving photographs of high flat interiors tend to show cosy living rooms with easy chairs in front of the electric fire and an array of decorative embellishments. Figure 2.1 is a good example of such representations. But it is likely that some flats would have been sparsely furnished when new tenants moved in. Brian, who moved to the Gorbals in 1965, remarked that he was 'probably seventeen before we had a carpet' and similarly Mr Goldie who spent some years as a child at Moss Heights recalled linoleum floor coverings which shamed his parents:

> Even me, ah was never encouraged to bring friends in, ah did, you know, ah was allowed to at times but it was never really encouraged an' sometimes they would say don't bring anyone in or you go out an' play if you want but don't bring people in. An' maybe, so it depends on how they felt about their house or whether they thought it wis, eh, up to the standard of other people's houses you know. Ah mean, there was a time when people started to get fitted carpets in the late sixties, but that was in advance of just a kind of linoleum floor wae a kind o' carpet on it, so some people might think, oh we don't have a fitted carpet you know, we can't let them in here, you know, so there's a kind of, you know, embarrassment about it. Ah remember when we finally got one ah felt more secure then because ah sort of thought well we've got a fitted carpet at last, you know so, if anybody comes in we can't be you know, ashamed for having linoleum floors an' bits of carpets.[59]

Cheaper tufted carpets were part of the late 1950s and early 60s consumer boom – these were less expensive than the traditional woven woollen carpets and were aggressively advertised to the working classes who had hitherto made do with linoleum and assorted rag rugs.[60] This meant that for many the carpet became the marker of respectability and, as in the case of Tricia's mother in Castlemilk, had to be protected from wear – 'to protect the new carpet she had lots o' rugs down'.[61] In the Spence-designed blocks in Queen Elizabeth Square on the other hand, the linoleum which came with the flats had been designed specifically and Paul's mother preferred to keep it. 'It just made the place feel airy; you didn't have that carpet thing going on to densify it down.'[62]

Notions of 'respectability' and 'having things nice' or up to date could be achieved with the aid of credit or hire purchase schemes. John and Carol, a young couple who moved from a single-end tenement apartment to a flat in Castlemilk in 1969, described how they furnished their home with fashionable items purchased using a local store's hire purchase arrangement:

JOHN: London Road in Gallowgate, and it used to be a big furniture shop. And what you had was … you looked in the window, and each window had a different set-up and it had like a carpet and a bedroom suite, and it was an all-inclusive price tag, you know, whatever, it was £199 or whatever, would it have been as much as that in those days? So Carol and I used to have our faces pressed up against this, like kids in a sweetie shop you know and we'd say 'I want that one', and we'd go in and you could pay this up, you know, so we had our room kitted out.

CAROL: That was after we paid the suite off.

JOHN: After we paid the suite off. And then we had the one room and then we managed to pay that out, we'd go back down and look in the window again and then get another lot.

CAROL: The kids' room.

JOHN: And that suite would go into the kids' room. And that's how we did it.[63]

Others saved up to equip their homes with modern labour saving and leisure items such as twin-tub washing machines and refrigerators, radio-grams, sideboards, coffee tables, record players, televisions and sun-loungers (for the veranda) or used saving schemes operated by some of the larger stores. Lorraine recalled, 'that was the first time we got a colour telly which was doon at the shops. So ah think they paid it up weekly'.[64] John and Carol described such a 'menage' (savings club) that enabled them to purchase a set of fashionable lamps:

so we used to save up, you know and give her our menage money every week and everybody in the flats must have had this set of lamps. A standard lamp, it was a table lamp and you know these tall ash-trays? It must have been all the same set. You could either get it in an orange colour or a yellow colour, but everybody had the same lamps (laughing) everything the same.[65]

And of course the purchase of these consumer goods both reflected and supported a new pattern of family life which was more home focused than might hitherto have been the case when homes were cold, cramped, damp and lacking basic facilities.

John and Carol had very little furniture of their own when they moved in but they soon set about personalising their brand new home in a style that suited the modern space as well as their limited finances:

JOHN: … It was really spartan at the time, and some … when we moved up the flats it was a whole new life-style you know. We had all these empty rooms and a bed, so we had to actually save up for …

CAROL: An Orbit suite.

JOHN: An Orbit suite it was called, it was a three piece suite, and it was like the … getting on for the late 60s by this time, so it was like space-age design you know, it was bucket chairs that swivelled round, and this … this couch that probably wouldn't be allowed to be manufactured nowadays (laughter) certainly wouldn't be fire retardant or anything.

CAROL: No.

JOHN: So that was our first purchase.

CAROL: Oh and the horse, your rocking horse that we took the rocking … well when the wee one was finished with it, we made it into a coffee table (laughing).

JOHN: Aye, I made it into a coffee table. I used to like doing things like that, we actually had a bar in the living room.

CAROL: Made it out of a wardrobe on its side, it was lovely.

JOHN: It never had any drink in it. All our relatives called it the pub with no beer!

CAROL: And then we kind of grew out of the bar and you made, you started to make book cases, and you made, erm, what was it, the fireplace.[66]

This couple are unusual in being able to recall in such detail their efforts to personalise their flat; also noticeable is that they consciously, at the time and in retrospect, recall their desire to be modern. Carol expressed pride in her kitchen and recalled making coordinating accessories. But it was the living room that was most expressive of their modern aesthetic:

> But my living room was, I thought it was gorgeous … and I had a lovely little table that we had our Trimphone on, because we managed to get a 'phone which I had to wait a million years for, it was one of these nice wee Trimphones, and John and I were just reminiscing the other day about our radiogram that we had. It was a long wooden radiogram and that's where you had your LPs and your singles and everything, and that was fabulous … and I thought my house was fabulous, I really did (laughing). Of course I told you about the lamps, you know, the standard lamp, the table lamp and the big ash tray, all matching you know. So that was my house …[67]

Although there may have been fewer DIY opportunities in high flats compared with other types of new dwelling – there were no sheds or workshops or easy access to outside space – John was not unusual in turning his hand to home improvement to achieve the look they desired.[68] Tricia who moved to Castlemilk with her family in the 1960s also recalled her father making some adjustments to the interior bathroom in their flat:

The bathroom had no window in it, em, 'cause it was in the flat, so it was midway up the hall on the left hand side in our case an' it just had the toilet wash hand basin an' then the bath. An' my dad, my mum put a glass door in the bathroom because there was no window in it ... She figured that would be good, so we had this glass door which was quite kind of out there in the sixties. And em, my dad tiled it in yellow and white tiles, the whole bathroom, put little glass mounted, little glass shelves for wur toothbrush an' aw ae that. It was, it was quite snazzy, eh, and we really, really enjoyed it.[69]

People's enjoyment of their flats and pride in making them look nice demonstrates active home-making and identification with the home notwithstanding the fact that they were tenants not owners. Tricia, was clear about this:

People spent a fortune in their houses to have them all dickied up in the best of stuff.... It was your house.... Yip, you decorated it, you kept it clean, you know like, they put up all fancy wall paper, they, as ah say they carpeted it, got fancy lights, you know like, it was their house, it wisnae a council house. So, it's different from now where people, you know when they rent a place they, you know the landlord does all the painting an', it wasn't that case at all, the council handed it over to you and it was yours.[70]

Similarly Paul recalled his mother's enjoyment of modern design and her constant efforts to update their flat:

My mum oh my god my mother, I don't think I can remember one particular style that woman had.... She changed the look of that place every week.... She was always buying and spending a small fortune on a new ornament.... She was of the time. I do remember she had a wee penchant for Habitat you know working class shouldn't be shopping in Habitat at the time but yes she constantly was and she was very DIY about stuff always, week to week we would go in and the settee would be in a different area, she would build stuff. Because the innards of the flats were quite flexible and open plan so you could effectively get away with doing that because the light was so good.[71]

High flat residents in the 1960s and 70s set about personalising their homes once they obtained public as opposed to private tenancies and their efforts were enabled by the growth and availability of home furnishings and access to finance. Although some tried to recreate what they were used to in older style dwellings, many young families embraced the new to align with the modernity of the flat and regarded their home as a means to 'express the fullness of their lives'.[72]

Privacy versus communality

Many residents were happy to close their door on the world and enjoy their modern home, the benefits of the interior outweighing dislike of the block's design: as one young female resident put it: 'it is the inside that counts'.[73] Yet whilst high-rise blocks facilitated the privacy of family life in ways that many appreciated, at the same time high density living required a degree of communality and cooperation amongst residents and high maintenance standards from the landlord. When conditions within the blocks deteriorated – when lifts broke down, when outsiders made incursions into the blocks or when residents failed to adhere to common norms of behaviour – people experienced anxiety and dissatisfaction and retreated from the communal life of the block. This section considers the tensions created by communal spaces – lifts, stairwells, corridors – and addresses design issues, inadequate maintenance and the dysfunctional communality that was the result in many cases.

Architects had envisioned the shared interior spaces of the block – the corridors, entrance halls and lifts – as mimicking the street life of traditional communities, creating opportunities for neighbourliness, cooperation and casual interaction. They assumed moreover, that those used to living in crowded tenements where cooperation was essential, especially amongst women, would easily adapt to the high flats. But although residents were able to create a home behind their front door, they had little power when it came to the wider communal environment of the block which could house more than 100 separate households. Mrs Andrews, who had moved to Castlemilk from another peripheral estate to be near her daughter in 1965, clearly articulated her concerns about noise, nuisance and insecurity:

> I don't like so many people around me and there's an awful lot of children around. You don't know when your house is going to be broken into – there's an awful lot of it around. The noise travels up a lot. The children play outside the back entrance and the noise is very bad. There is a terrible noise from the lifts – can't get to sleep for it at night. These houses aren't soundproofed. I can hear the man on the 11th floor playing his piano and the man underneath us is deaf and I can hear every word that is said to him.[74]

Noisy lifts and rubbish chutes were a frequent cause of complaint in some blocks, an indicator of how satisfactory high density, high-rise living was dependent upon design as well as consideration for others and not just those living adjacent. Mrs Shea, a 68-year-old widow, remarked in 1968 so early in the life of the flats, that the rubbish chute was 'only supposed to be used at certain times but it's used at any old times. They don't bother'.[75] This was a widespread problem and not just for older people. 'I can't use my bedroom because it is near to the garbage chute! It is only supposed to be used from 8 am to 8 pm but there's always someone using it late hours and early morning' commented a mother of three.[76] Residents' lack of consideration for neighbours in their use of communal resources could lead to misery for individuals in their own homes and conversely, the flats were often cramped, and mothers were anxious about their children disturbing neighbours with their noise. 'The noise carries' commented a housewife from Castlemilk.

> I can hear my neighbour's radio and I was glad to get out and get a job! My girl goes to ballet dancing and I'm reluctant to let her practice and also I don't let her practice the piano. The older ones – I can tell not to run and jump but the younger ones tend to run and jump! A good feature is the verandah. You need that! In the summer I get through my housework and shopping then sit and knit out on it. For people with babies in prams it's a must![77]

Although the flats were trumpeted as being a 'housewife's dream', it soon became evident that they presented even greater challenges than the tyranny of the tenement with its shared chores and inadequate facilities. The post-war privatised family that sought its refuge in the home, ate together and increasingly spent its leisure time together was dependent on women's unpaid work. Communal facilities for cooking or child care that might have released women from their individual responsibilities were never implemented in block designs meaning that this form of housing in particular served to isolate women in domesticity, especially if they had pre-school children.[78] Privacy for some women became imprisonment. 'The women are really prisoners from one weekend to the other' remarked a male Wyndford resident.[79] Jephcott was alert to the potential for high flats to trap women in an environment which accentuated their containment indoors and hindered casual social contact, especially those traditional forms well known in Glasgow such as 'window-hinging', stair-nattering and sitting out on the pavement on a summer day.[80] At the same time, however, women were still responsible for keeping the communal areas of the block clean. Female residents in particular complained about the difficulty they had in cleaning the windows and undertaking other communal chores.

> We have far too many windows and outside work to do. We have to wash the fire escape verandah and all the woodwork and windows and we have 3 glass panelled doors we have to wash. We have about 8 inside landing windows to wash.[81]

Housework undertaken within the flat was not conspicuous – no-one would see the white window nets or the washing blowing on the line – so those who did take pride in housework took the opportunity when asked to emphasise the work they did to keep the communal areas clean.[82]

Lorraine recalled a competitive respectability at work as her mother would often say: '"Oh, hiv ye seen that landin?" or, you know, so obviously there wis wans that didn't ...'[83] Many women had anticipated an escape from the cleaning and laundry rotas in tenements but the demands of keeping these buildings clean just reinforced women's responsibility for housework. Residents who refused to undertake their share of the communal chores also broke the fragile co-existence on floors which could contain anything from six flats to as many as fourteen.[84] And if maintaining cleanliness and respectability in the block was challenging in the early decades, it became almost impossible as the constituency of blocks changed, when caretakers were withdrawn leaving chute rooms filthy and landings uncleaned. Lorraine described the situation in Castlemilk that contributed to her mother deciding to leave the high flats in the 1980s:

> An' then people wurnae looking efter the, the landins, an' ah don't know why they changed the pensioners, see it wis always pensioners houses an' then they started jist putting single people in them, so they were any age. That didnae work very well ah don't think either. You know the whole point ae it, ah always thought it wis quite, well when ah think aboot it noo, ah mean you knew theym an' if they needed anything you always knew who stayed in your landin. Ah dae remember getting sent tae see wee Mrs so-and-so is awright, or if she needs anything. So that wis a whole community thing an' everybody as far as ah know, mah friends as well, you always knew who yer, who the wee man wis, who the wee wummin wis that stayed in yer landin.

Lorraine's mother had developed good social relations with her neighbours over more than a decade. But, in the early days of the flats, women in particular remarked on the ways in which the block design inhibited social contact. Long corridors militated against neighbourliness and exacerbated feelings of isolation for old and young alike. An 82 year old widow living in Queen Elizabeth Square in the Gorbals suggested 'it is too quiet, the corridors are too long, can't get to know people'.[85] Asked if she was satisfied, she replied: 'I wish I was back in my wee room and kitchen where you were able to meet people and you knew everybody round about. Here you don't know a soul and nobody bothers about you'.[86] Younger tenants also found it 'impersonal' with a 20-year-old woman who lived with her brother stating that 'You see hundreds of people but you don't know them. It is like a hostel or hospital with the long corridors'.[87]

The design of high-rise blocks seems to have inhibited casual interactions which, over time affected people's (especially women's) communal commitments to its upkeep. For Helen who moved to Queen Elizabeth Square in the Gorbals in 1965 as a child:

> the deterioration started when the stairs began to smell we found out people were using it as a public toilet. So with nobody keeping an eye on it people could go in there and not even be seen so they would be peeing in it and other things and graffiti. It was the same with the lifts; you would walk in the lifts and what used to be a nice shiny lift I used to hate it. You would just stand there and I used to hate it there would be urine on the floor – it got to the point I was embarrassed to take people back there and that was only in a period of what five years. I do believe that was because nobody could look out the window and see people; all you could see was outside not internally. That allowed anybody to come in and do what they wanted and it got to the stage where I was quite scared to go down the steps you never knew who you would come across and that was before the drugs really started taking shape.[88]

Helen's mother, who was so delighted at the new Queen Elizabeth Square flat in 1965, eventually moved out in the 1980s. Helen, who had moved away and spent considerable time overseas, was concerned about her mother's mental health, and on one occasion resorted to phoning the local priest from Hong Kong to ask for someone to check on her mother's well-being. She believed her mother was depressed. She would say 'I hate this place, I just want to get away from it because it's [such a] closed feeling'. Upon moving to a three-bedroomed flat with access to a garden 'She was like a new woman as soon as she got out of there.'[89]

Tricia, whose family moved to Castlemilk in 1966, explained that after the 'honeymoon period' people began to move on 'and as people moved, quite quickly ... it was total strangers you were living with'. It then became difficult to maintain collective routines based on respectability such as the cleaning of landings, stairs and rubbish chutes. While in some blocks this had always been an issue, there was a perception of change in the 1970s, a theme that is further elaborated in Chapter 4. Tricia recalled that her chore was to clean the stairs on a Friday night and 'ye could hear all the women out washin'. But 'in the end there was only, from eight going down, there was only ... six that were getting done. And the rest weren't. So you can picture how filthy they were'. This was accompanied by what Tricia described as 'this kind of silence': neighbours stopped chatting when waiting for the lift.

> [Y]ou would go in an' people, we would all be standing there, we're all neighbours in the one building an' now even people that in the beginning you were kind of nodding to, because you haven't seen them in six months you maybe can't remember their name....

Eventually her parents moved out of the block following a break in; her mother was convinced it was people living in the block and 'she was never right after that ... I don't think she ever recovered from that'.[90]

Maintenance and security

Tricia's observations about the decline of standards and feelings of insecurity highlights the importance of the functional integrity of the block. One of the keys to this was working lifts. Jephcott suggested that 'every tenant had something to say' about them giving 'a strong impression that a lift-ridden existence added to the strains of daily life' as a result of their 'unpredictability'.[91] A survey conducted on lift waiting times on five estates revealed only Wyndford offered a satisfactory service whereas the 31-storey Red Road flats received a 'distinctly unsatisfactory' service owing to the number of stops, repeated vandalism and heavy usage.[92] Generally however, residents were of the opinion that the lifts were 'inadequate'.[93] The demand for lifts at peak periods such as first thing in the morning, especially with milkmen and paper boys using them, could result in having to 'wait ages to get them sometimes and can miss buses through them'.[94] Their size meant that 'a woman with a pram has great difficulty getting into the lift at busy times' and 'If there's a pram in it, and you're waiting with yours you've to wait until it goes down and back up again'.[95] Several people commented on the difficulty of transporting coffins as a 29 year old woman stated: 'I went into the lift once and the coffin was standing on end in it!'[96] There was also the issue of cleanliness, a problem that was to intensify over time: 'If you go down in the lifts late Saturday or early Sunday it's flooded just with drunks using it as a toilet'.[97] This was a common complaint in high rises across the city and near identical comments feature in all of our case study areas. In fact the persistent failure, vandalism and misuse of lifts became symbolic of the later decline in high rise in the 1980s in Glasgow and other cities.

Anxiety about the lifts was just one element of wider concerns about the safety and general environment of the block. It is notable that where caretakers were resident (they tended to be responsible for several blocks on an estate) they countered the impersonal and alienating features of the towers and residents' had a sense of pride and felt safe.[98] From policing of anti-social behaviour to ensuring tenants were taking their turn of cleaning communal areas, caretakers helped to create a culture in a block which fostered communality. As Jephcott argued when making the case for increased investment in staff in high rise, the caretaker played 'a vital part in the life of every tenant'.[99] 'We don't have much trouble here – there's a very good caretaker. You can come out and in and there's no anybody bother you' remarked a 50-year old widow in Castlemilk.[100] It is notable that after years of neglect, in the 1990s concierge and security guards were employed in high-rise blocks to address 'unsociable behaviour'.

Conclusions

For Jephcott, 'the households most likely to make a success of a multi-storey life were those whose interests did not centre on the home', who had plenty of personal resources and were relatively well-educated and well-off.[101] This contradicts the intentions of those who championed the flats as ideal for the nuclear family and the inculcation of domestic privacy. Our consideration of social relations inside the block suggests a more nuanced picture. For many new residents in the 1960s and 1970s the high-rise flat was one stage in a housing journey which took them away from overcrowded slum accommodation. People's delight at their modern, well-equipped homes and their desire to create an environment where they could achieve domestic privacy should be understood in this context. Our focus here on the everyday – use of the veranda, home décor, cleaning the stairs – offers a reading of high-rise life in Glasgow which suggests the 'failure narrative' requires a closer look. Both the immediate impressions of life in a high-rise flat gathered by Jephcott in the 1960s and the memories recounted some 50 years later show mixed responses to living high, but a common theme is the embrace of domestic privacy initially because so many were relieved to escape the 'inescapable togetherness' of past housing. In the short term the high flats met this need. While not all were content on high-rise estates, few were discontented with their homes and many gained pleasure in them. Later, however, as conditions in the block and on the estate (as we shall see in Chapters 3 and 4) caused anxiety, the domestic retreat was transformed into a refuge from the world outside. As Helen explained when asked to reflect on her time in Queen Elizabeth Square: 'The flats didn't give you [community], they were built so you could shut the door and cut the world off and that's you – you are safe from everybody but that's not a way to live.'[102] The high flats could only be a success for residents when the individual in his or her flat felt at ease in the community of the block and by extension also a belonging to the environment of the estate. It is to the outside that we turn our attention in Chapter 3.

Notes

1 Studies of modern homes that consider the interior include: Nicole C.Rudolph, *At Home in Postwar France. Modern Mass Housing and the Right to Comfort* (Berghahn, New York, 2015); Attfield, *Bringing Modernity Home*; Ben Highmore, *The Great Indoors. At Home in the Modern British House* (Profile Books, London. 2014). For an earlier period see Jane Hamlett, *Material Relations: Domestic Interiors and Middle-Class Families in England, 1850–1910* (Manchester University Press, Manchester, 2010).
2 Jephcott's comments tend to focus on amenity, what she described as 'physical character'. *Homes in High Flats*, pp. 48–58.
3 Examples include Glendinning and Muthesius, *Tower Block*; Horsey, *Tenements and Towers*; Miles Glendinning (ed.), *Rebuilding Scotland: the Postwar Vision 1945–1975* (Tuckwell Press, Edinburgh, 1997); Dunleavy, *The Politics of Mass Housing in Britain*; Phil Jones, 'The suburban high flat in the postwar reconstruction of Birmingham, 1945–71', *Urban History* 32:2 (2005), pp. 323–41.
4 Coleman, *Utopia on Trial*; Hanley, *Estates*.
5 Jephcott, *Homes in High Flats*, p. 107.
6 National Library of Scotland, Moving Image Archive: 'Mungo's Medals'. Public Information film produced by Glasgow Corporation, 1961. The film can be viewed at http://movingimage.nls.uk
7 On the idea of the post-war home as the fulcrum of the privatised family and the high-rise flat as the most extreme example see Tim Newton and Charles Putnam (eds), *Household Choices* (Futures Publications, Middlesex, 1990). A survey by Glasgow council in 1943 revealed a majority of householders were in favour of a bungalow or cottage-style home. This preference was ignored by Glasgow Corporation's housing committee chair who referred to the 'wastage of land on cottage-style houses'. *Housing in 20th Century Glasgow: Documents 1914–1990s* (Glasgow, 1996), pp. 123–5 and 156.
8 Parker Morris, *Homes for Today and Tomorrow* (HMSO, London, 1961), p. 3.
9 HES: MS 2329/X/19/17 (Basil Spence collection), letter from Spence to Ada Louise Huxtable, *New York Times*, 1 November 1965.
10 Grindrod, *Concretopia*, pp. 336–8 on structural failings of Glasgow high flats.
11 Daniel Miller, 'Appropriation of the state on the council estate', *Man*, New series 23:2 (1988), pp. 353–72; Judith Attfield, 'Bringing modernity home:

open plan in the British domestic interior' in Irene Cieraad (ed.), *At Home: An Anthropology of Domestic Space* (New York, 1999), pp. 73–82.

12 Glendinning and Muthesius, *Tower Block*, p. 14. Letter to chair, Glasgow housing committee, 1962 in *Housing in 20th Century Glasgow*, p. 154.

13 This follows the approach of Judith Attfield, 'Design as a practice of Modernity: a case for the study of the coffee table in the mid-century domestic interior', *Journal of Material Culture* 2:3 (1997), pp. 267–89, here 267–70.

14 Glendinning and Muthesius, *Tower Block*, pp. 14–15.

15 UGA, DC 127/13/1 1967–68, Miscellaneous documents: Glasgow Corporation, *Notes for Guidance of Tenants*.

16 National Records of Scotland, DD6/4459: Multi-Storey Flats General and Red Road 1958–79, Housing Development Group comments on Red Road flats, 16 October 1961.

17 See Glendinning and Muthesius, *Tower Block*, p. 12.

18 HES: Basil Spence papers: MS 2329/STC/37/2, letter from Spence to Peter Ferguson, 1963/4 (undated).

19 HES: Basil Spence papers, MS2329/STC/37/1, *Scottish Daily Express* (undated).

20 Jephcott, *Homes in High Flats*, pp. 48–53.

21 UGA, DC 127/1/1-10/1: Questionnaire for the statistical study of the social implications of domestic housing in multi-storey flats, including contact sheets – Castlemilk (hereafter UGA DC 127/1/1-10/1). All respondents' names in the text have been anonymised with pseudonyms.

22 UGA, DC 127/1/1-10/1, Castlemilk.

23 UGA, DC 127/1/1-10/1, Castlemilk.

24 Interview with Mr Leslie Welch (Moss Heights, b.1950), 2015.

25 Ibid.

26 Interview with Isabelle (Castlemilk, b.1952), 2015.

27 Interview with John and Carol (Castlemilk, b.1947), 2015.

28 Interview with Brian (Queen Elizabeth Square, Gorbals, b.c.1960), 2015.

29 Jephcott's study asked all respondents to say whether they were 'satisfied' or 'unsatisfied' with their home – 91 per cent responded positively. Jephcott, *Homes in High Flats*, p. 176. For an analysis of Jephcott's research methodology see Barry Hazley, Valerie Wright, Lynn Abrams, Ade Kearns, '"People and their homes rather than housing in the usual sense"? Locating the tenant's voice in *Homes in High Flats*', *Women's History Review*, 28:5 (2019), pp. 728–45.

30 Interview with Lorraine (Castlemilk, b.1964), 2015.

31 Judith Attfield, 'Inside pram town: a case study of Harlow house interiors 1951–1961', in Judith Attfield and Pat Kirkham (eds), *A View from the Interior: Feminism, Women and Design* (Women's Press, London, 2nd ed., 1995).

32 Clive Edwards, *Turning Houses into Homes. A History of the Retailing and Consumption of Domestic Furnishings* (Ashgate, Aldershot, 2005), p. 214.

33 Jephcott, *Homes in High Flats*, Table 14, p. 173.

34 See Alison Ravetz and Richard Turkington, *The Place of Home* (Routledge, London, 1995), p. 57.

35 Interview with Tricia (Castlemilk, b.1957), 2015.

36 UGA, DC127/1/1-10/1: Moss Heights.

37 Interview with Mrs Mary Thallon (Moss Heights, b.1924), 2015.

38 Interview with Mrs Carol Brown (Moss Heights, b.1953), 2015.

39 Glendinning and Muthesius, *Tower Block*, p. 42.
40 Grindrod, *Concretopia*, p. 158.
41 UGA, DC127/1/1-10/1: Gorbals.
42 Interview with Mrs Betty Williamson (Wyndford, b.c.1950), 2015.
43 Interview with Tricia (Castlemilk, b.1957), 2015.
44 UGA, DC 127/1/1-10/1: Castlemilk.
45 Interview with Paul (Queen Elizabeth Square, Gorbals, b.1960), 2015. For another description of the uses of the veranda see the testimony of Eddie McGonnell in Grindrod, *Conretopia*, p. 158.
46 Interview with Mrs Carol Brown (Moss Heights, b.1953), 2015.
47 Interview with John and Carol (Castlemilk, b.1947), 2015.
48 Interview with Isabelle (Castlemilk, b.1952), 2015.
49 Interview with Tricia (Castlemilk. b.1957), 2015.
50 UGA, DC 127/1/1-10/1: Castlemilk.
51 UGA, DC 127/1/1-10/1: Castlemilk.
52 UGA, DC 127/1/1-10/1: Castlemilk.
53 Interview with Tricia (Castlemilk, b.1957), 2015.
54 UGA, DC 127/1/1-10/1: Castlemilk.
55 UGA, DC 127/1/1-10/1: Gorbals.
56 UGA, DC 127/1/1-10/1: Castlemilk.
57 See Edwards, *Turning Houses into Homes,* pp. 173–247; Judith Attfield, 'The tufted carpet in Britain: its rise from the bottom of the pile', *Journal of Design History*, 9:3 (1994), pp. 205–16.
58 Jephcott, *Homes in High Flats*, p. 175.
59 Interview with Mr Ray Goldie (Moss Heights, b.1951), 2015.
60 Attfield, 'The tufted carpet'.
61 Interview with Tricia (Castlemilk, b.1957), 2015.
62 Interview with Paul (Gorbals, b.1960), 2015.
63 Interview with John and Carol (Castlemilk, b.1947), 2015.
64 Interview with Lorraine (Castlemilk, b.1964), 2015.
65 Interview with John and Carol (Castlemilk, b.1947), 2015.
66 Interview with John and Carol (Castlemilk, b.1947), 2015.
67 Interview with John and Carol (Castlemilk, b.1947), 2015.
68 For a discussion of DIY in another Scottish context, the new town, see Lynn Abrams, Barry Hazley, Valerie Wright, Ade Kearns. 'Aspiration, agency and the production of new selves in a Scottish new town *c*.1947–*c*.2016', *Twentieth Century British History* 29:4 (2018), pp. 576–604. And see Jephcott *Homes in High Flats*, p. 103. Interview with Tricia (Castlemilk, b.1957), 2015.
69 Ibid.
70 Interview with Tricia (Castlemilk, b.1957), 2015.
71 Interview with Paul (Gorbals, b.1960), 2015
72 Parker Morris, *Homes for Today and Tomorrow*, p. 3.
73 UGA, DC 127/1/1-10/1: Gorbals.
74 UGA, DC 127/1/1-10/1: Castlemilk.
75 UGA, DC 127/1/1-10/1: Castlemilk.
76 UGA, DC 127/1/1-10/1: Castlemilk.
77 UGA, DC 127/1/1-10/1: Castlemilk.
78 In countries where communal facilities were mooted or provided, residents were generally resistant to sharing. See Rudolph, *At Home in Postwar France*,

p. 139; Lynne Attwood, *Gender and Housing in Soviet Russia: Private Life in a Public Space* (Manchester University Press, Manchester, 2010), pp. 63–71.

79 UGA, DC 127/1/1-10/1: Wyndford.
80 Jephcott, *Homes in High Flats*, p. 110.
81 UGA, DC 127/1/1-10/1: Wyndford.
82 Attfield, 'Inside pram town', p. 234.
83 Interview with Lorraine (Castlemilk, b.1964), 2015.
84 The most common number of flats per floor was six but one block had 28 per floor split level. Jephcott, *Homes in High Flats*, p. 38.
85 UGA, DC 127/1/1-10/1: Gorbals.
86 UGA, DC 127/1/1-10/1: Gorbals.
87 UGA, DC 127/1/1-10/1: Gorbals.
88 Interview with Helen (Gorbals, b.1954), 2015.
89 Interview with Helen (Gorbals, b.1954), 2015.
90 Interview with Tricia (Castlemilk, b.1957), 2015.
91 Jephcott, *Homes in High Flats*, p. 55.
92 Jephcott, *Homes in High Flats*, pp. 162–3.
93 UGA, DC 127/1/1-10/1: Castlemilk.
94 UGA, DC 127/1/1-10/1: Castlemilk.
95 UGA, DC 127/1/1-10/1: Castlemilk.
96 UGA, DC 127/1/1-10/1: Castlemilk.
97 UGA, DC 127/1/1-10/1: Castlemilk.
98 Jephcott, *Homes in High Flats*, p. 119.
99 Jephcott, *Homes in High Flats*, p. 120.
100 UGA, DC 127/1/1-10/1: Castlemilk.
101 Jephcott, *Homes in High Flats*, p. 105.
102 Interview with Helen (Gorbals, b.1954), 2015.

3 Outside

Surviving and thriving on estates

The opportunity to create a cosy retreat in a modern flat was embraced by the majority of residents, but outside the walls of the block it was more difficult to adapt to an environment which could be aesthetically alienating, lacking amenities and, unlike a street, not always conducive to the establishment of common norms of behaviour or casual social interaction. In Glasgow the high-rise construction drive of the 1960s has come to be associated in the popular imagination with municipal vandalism and planning failure symbolised by representations of rundown, windswept estates.[1] Both the design of the estate and its location were often blamed for causing, or at the very least exacerbating, the social marginalisation of the high flats' residents and ultimately social breakdown in those communities. The reality was far more complicated.

While the brutalist design of many high-rise estates had serious consequences for some groups – mothers with young children and older residents in particular – it is too simplistic to draw direct connections between design and planning on these estates and urban deprivation, 'problem families' and a plethora of social issues such as high unemployment, drug and alcohol dependency, criminality and violence.[2] Planning and design did matter, but in this chapter we show how the design and maintenance of the environment around the high flats was perceived and experienced very differently by men and women and different age groups and was not the only factor determining whether residents thrived or merely survived.

Paying attention to issues such as estate management and upkeep, the provision of amenities and services and security is important because the viability of the high-rise experiment rested not only on the provision of new homes but on the remaking of communities. A modern home and the privacy that the flat provided were key elements desired by many high-rise residents but privacy could easily turn into isolation and refuge in the absence of a sustaining environment outside the flat. While relocation to a high-rise estate was not always accompanied by the break up of communities – many of the first residents of the Gorbals high flats moved together from demolished streets in the vicinity of the new estate for instance – nevertheless, the remaking of communities, albeit less cheek-by-jowl and more desirous of household privacy, required significant investment in essential services and amenities such as shops, transport and social venues for both genders and all age groups.

During the construction of new housing estates in the immediate post-war decades concerns were expressed about the planning and layout of the outdoor shared communal spaces.[3] Research on perceived planning failures began in the early 1950s and continued throughout the main period of high-rise construction in the 1960s and beyond. The spaces surrounding high-rise blocks were thought to be particularly problematic, with many commentators having an aversion to the modernist, or more accurately 'brutalist', aesthetic.[4] Contemporary studies undertaken throughout the UK in the 1960s and 1970s underlined the complexity of problems affecting the environmental quality of housing estates with particular concerns about play facilities, vandalism and unsatisfactory amenity provision.[5] From the early 1970s onwards the residualisation of council housing meant high-rise communities on many estates became less stable and investment in maintenance and amenity provision stalled.[6] The resultant effect for longer term residents was the retreat from communality as opportunities for casual sociability declined, imprisonment in the flat, and for many a move elsewhere.

In this chapter we will focus on two estates which have become emblematic of 'planning failure' in Glasgow: the inner city area of the Gorbals, and the peripheral estate of Castlemilk. Both had historically negative reputations prior to the building of high flats which explains why there was an attempt to redevelop and add prestige with high-rise blocks in the 1960s. Queen Elizabeth Square replaced nineteenth century slum tenements in the Gorbals, an area long associated with crime and vice and Glasgow's 'no mean city' reputation.[7] In Castlemilk, five systems-built point blocks were added on the southernmost edge of the already geographically isolated estate on high ground near the hills of the Cathkin Braes which ensured they could be seen on the horizon from all over the city.[8] These particular blocks were therefore a symbolic and powerful message to Glasgow citizens that the Corporation was tackling the city's housing crisis. Beyond their rhetorical importance however, the location of these blocks and the estate of which they were a part, especially the distance from the city centre, were significant in influencing residents' opinions of the outdoor spaces on their estate, as were the level of amenities and maintenance provided. This did not turn out to be the case in the Gorbals. First, we consider the views of residents expressed in the late

1960s on the outdoor spaces and environment of the estates, including their reflections on geographical location and the provision of amenities and facilities. Then we turn to the contrasting perceptions of adults and children on the suitability of high-rise estates for children with adults fearing the outside and children relishing its freedoms.

Estate planning, amenity and social life

For Glasgow's high-rise residents in the 1960s location was important, as was the planning and provision of amenities, as these factors affected how people reflected on the outdoor spaces in the immediate vicinity of the block, the neighbourhood and estate as a whole. On the periphery of the city in Castlemilk residents noted the benefits of their proximity to the open space of the nearby hills and the 'fresh air'. As Mr Cable stated 'When you go into the town you're glad to get back – you feel tied in the town'.[9] However, these residents were also severely disadvantaged by the distance of the towers from the central shopping area in Castlemilk as well as the city centre. The estate's lack of amenities in terms of social facilities or regular and reliable public transport was problematic. The resources provided for residents were simply not commensurate with the spatial scale and population of the estate which comprised around 40,000 people. When Jephcott surveyed the estate she counted just two shops within a ten-minute walk of the high flats. The high-rise estate was also poorly served with recreational provision – there was no pub within half a mile, few sports' facilities or social provision, and compared with city-centre locations the high-rise blocks in Castlemilk lacked easily accessible services such as a doctor's surgery, dentist and child welfare clinic.[10] In the inner city Gorbals some residents did not take to the concrete brutalist design of the redeveloped area, illustrated in Figure 3.1, with many describing Queen Elizabeth Square as 'institutional' or 'prison' like.[11] The redeveloped Gorbals certainly lacked greenspace. But a more holistic planning strategy in terms of the provision of local amenities and shopping facilities, as well as the central location, was some form of compensation here. The problems associated with lack of amenities and isolation of peripheral estates were well established in both the national and local media by the late 1960s, and the critique of the alienating effects of brutalist architecture and concrete was already developing too, which undoubtedly affected the perceptions of residents when they were asked their views by Jephcott's research team.[12]

Almost 50 years on, some who grew up in Castlemilk and the Gorbals in the 1960s and 1970s were defensive of the aims of planners and architects and were proud of their flats standing tall on the horizon. Lorraine,

Figure 3.1 Hutchesontown 'C' (Queen Elizabeth Square) in the Gorbals showing the pilotis (stilts) at the base of the blocks.

who lived in Castlemilk for 20 years, was typical of those interviewees who expressed a nostalgia for the high rise mixed with the simultaneous acknowledgement that it was not a good place to live:

Aye, but ah mean anywhere ye went ye could see them. Em, ah even remember mibbee when ah went on holiday ye know, an' you could always spot them when ye came intae Glesga airport, ye know, ye'd go, oh there's the flats. Em, well, mah da wid show me where, ah wid never remember, but he wid go, there're the flats [laughs]. Eh, but ah, ah don't remember a lot an' a never hid much mair tae kind of a do wae them, but yet, when they get pullt doon it wis really, oh [intake of breath], it wis quite, ah don't know, ah think ye jist thought ae yer childhood, ye know, an' ye thought, what a shame. That wis mah only reaction, ye know, that ye wid go, oh God we hid great times up there, so why did it end up that it wis jist brrr .You know there wis nothing an' people hated it an'.... Cause they wur, they wur completely, hit wis completely different, it wis completely, we wur just used tae oor place, an' where, where we lived.[13]

Brian who moved into Queen Elizabeth Square in 1965 simply stated that 'it wis sold as Utopia an' it, it really wisnae'.[14]

Life on the periphery: a lack of foresight

The failure of the Corporation's planners was obvious in the case of Glasgow's peripheral housing estates. The priority of David Gibson, the city's housing convenor, was to clear the slums and 'give the people homes'.[15] Such was the urgency of Glasgow's perpetual housing crisis, the emphasis was on housing alone and not on pioneering estate design or even on providing shops, schools, churches, community and sports centres. Residents in the peripheral estates had to campaign throughout the 1950s and 1960s for basic amenities and facilities to be constructed, a campaign that is ongoing. In 2019 Castlemilk residents were still lobbying for a supermarket to serve the 14,000 residents under the slogan 'It's not fair' and referencing the 75 minute walk to reach the nearest large store.[16] The Glaswegian comedian Billy Connolly who was relocated with his family to Drumchapel, another of Glasgow's peripheral estates, famously described these far-flung estates as 'deserts wae windaes'.[17] In a BBC documentary from 1965, a dissatisfied resident relocated to Castlemilk from the Gorbals described it as a 'barracks', somewhere you came home to sleep as there was nothing else to do.[18] Valerie Somerville, a post-graduate student working at the University of Glasgow, completed a short ethnographic survey of the high-rise blocks in Castlemilk in 1967 which remains illuminating despite the obvious social distance of the researcher:

The nearest shops are 13 minutes' walk downhill – therefore back uphill with shopping to carry. Even then there is only a butcher's, grocer's, post-office etc. The main shopping centre is nearly two miles away.... The atmosphere of the place was a bit depressing. There were a large number of children playing in the streets. This was very noisy and some of the bigger lads seemed a bit destructive. Although it was quite late, there were a good number of very young children in the street, quite a number probably under 5. These were mostly playing together but not with anything. There were a lot of older girls, say 11–16 yrs, standing around in closes or by gates alone, obviously not deigning to join in the play but probably with nothing else to do, nowhere to go. There seemed to be no café close at hand. There was a school in the immediate vicinity of the flats but no activities took place there in the evenings. There are two secondary schools – one Protestant, one Catholic in Castlemilk. There is one Church of Scotland, not too near the flats, and three Catholic churches, one of which is right next door.... There is some chalking on the walls, some pulling down of saplings, etc, but as yet no evidence of major vandalism. Litter is not extensive, though there seemed to be no litter bins. The flats and other houses do mean a lot of people living on top of one another though and the general dingy air of the place is not attractive.[19]

When offering their views to researchers in the 1960s, residents identified a number of key concerns: planning of the estate's layout, lack of public transport, lack of adequate provision for car parking, inadequate amenities and poor maintenance and upkeep. These concerns were refracted by gender. Female pedestrians were concerned with walking routes to schools and to the shops and with the inadequate public transport. In peripheral estates the unreliable bus service compounded residents', and especially women's, feelings that they were very much living on the edge of the city. There were only three bus services for the entire population of Castlemilk and only one service reached the high-rise blocks.[20] Mrs Holiday, a widow, simply stated that Castlemilk had 'too much walking in it and it was too expensive travelling in it!'[21] Residents of all ages shared the opinion that 'The buses are hopeless!' as 'you have to wait for hours' and then 'at busy times you can't get on!'.[22] 'This scheme's alright for them with cars' was one woman's pithy remark.[23] As a result many female residents were disadvantaged. Even though Mrs Thorn, a widow who walked with two sticks and described herself as 'crippled', thought it was 'beautiful in the summer', she noted that for 'the six months of the winter I'm completely shut in'.[24] Like the young mothers with prams, she found it difficult to walk up the steep slopes (as illustrated in Figure 3.2), especially in icy weather. The hilly topography had, according to another widow, Mrs Shea, resulted in 'lots of old people' moving out and 'they've taken kitchens again' moving back to room and kitchen flats in Victorian tenements in the inner city.[25] Other middle-aged residents were more pragmatic or perhaps conflicted in their views, with Mrs Richie stating that she would prefer to live nearer to her husband's work and 'it's the travelling to go anywhere',

Figure 3.2 Mitchelhill towers, Castlemilk showing the steep slope leading up to the entrance to the blocks.

but 'We've always lived in Castlemilk and like it. It's nice surroundings though. You can't have everything to suit you!'[26] Mrs Richie's comments express the central contradiction: residents liked the semi-rural setting of the high rise in Castlemilk but the distance from the city centre was a problem.

Unsurprisingly, the main planning failure for residents in the late 1960s was the lack of amenities provided, both in the area surrounding the high-rise blocks and in the estate as a whole. Again this isolation was felt differently and had varying practical consequences for women and men and also older residents. The peripheral location of the high-rise blocks was a particular burden for women, and young mothers especially, who overwhelmingly had responsibility for the daily grocery shopping. One of the inspirations for Glasgow's high rise, Le Corbusier's Unité d' habitation in Marseille, had two shopping streets built into the interior of the blocks, but this was never a feature of the derivative systems-built blocks in Glasgow and other British cities. The central shops on the estate were a 20-minute walk down hill and then back again. As one mother of two, stated

'I'm exhausted by half-way'.[27] Older residents, both male and female, commented on the problem young mothers and housewives had in terms of the lack of shops near the blocks and the limited variety of shops at the central shopping area in the estate, which meant that 'to really get a choice' they had to travel to the city centre.[28] The travelling grocery vans, which were a practical solution to this problem in all of Glasgow's peripheral estates, were also considered 'too dear' and 'did not provide a substitute for proper shops since they had limited stocks and were not suitable for more than the occasional purchase'.[29] Mrs McNair, a mother of two, liked Castlemilk and had requested 'to get up here' from the Gorbals in the inner city and particularly appreciated that there was 'lots of trees and a good view'. However, like many other women with young children living in the high-rise blocks in Castlemilk she felt it was 'a bit much to climb the hill heavily laden with shopping bags' and she especially hated 'pushing the pram up the hill'.[30] The benefits of the location of the blocks was yet again outweighed by the geographical isolation, in this case from everyday shopping facilities.[31]

Men, while just as critical of the estate layout and provision of amenities, had other priorities, namely the problems associated with car ownership on the estate. One resident suggested that the Corporation should provide more lock up garages as 'the cars are interfered with lying out and most folk own a car up here. They need it for the buses are not dependable'.[32] Car ownership probably reflected the location of the estate some miles from the city centre but it was overwhelmingly men who avoided the inconvenience of relying on buses. Tricia, who moved to the estate in the 1960s as a child, suggested that for her father, the move to high rise in Castlemilk in the 1966 was metaphorically, and quite literally, a move 'up in the world', but he was also a motorist and had one of the prized lock-up garages.[33] Female residents reliant on using poorly planned pathways to get around the estate on foot, as well as an undependable bus service for travelling further afield, felt quite differently.

Yet residents also complained about the Corporation's lack of maintenance of paths and greenspaces around the high blocks, and the estate as a whole. These greenspaces could be attractive in the summer when residents enjoyed the semi-rural location and views. However, when these spaces felt 'run-down' and neglected, this compounded the estate's negative reputation. It was therefore no surprise that as early as the 1960s residents commented on the estate's negative reputation as one of the city's much maligned four peripheral 'schemes'. People did not seem especially bothered by the 'dull layout' of many of the estates; after all the expanses of grass in Castlemilk were objectively more attractive than the environments many had experienced in the cramped neighbourhoods of the inner city. Yet residents were far more concerned with the perceived inadequate maintenance by the Corporation and neighbours not keeping up standards resulting in the area becoming 'down at heel'.[34] As Lawrence suggests in his study of post-war England, this was not new in the post-war years. Reputation had always mattered, with unofficial codes of 'respectable' behaviour being enforced by residents themselves in the 1920s and 1930s with regard to the use of the communal areas of the street.[35] This was especially true for the aspirational or 'respectable' working classes who aimed at 'improving standards' in areas of new housing to exceed what they had experienced before relocation.[36] Mrs Neil who had moved to the area in 1965 suggested that she had 'only heard stories about Castlemilk' and therefore 'didn't want to come', but that now she lived there she 'can't say anything against it'. Yet, she pointed out the failure of the Corporation to maintain shared public spaces complaining that there were not 'many street cleaners' and as a result 'sometimes the streets look pretty dirty – the back streets look as if they've never been brushed' as well as the 'few neglected gardens which don't make the place look as nice as it could'.[37]

The 'highly artificial character of the layout' on the high-rise estate including grass and concrete demanded 'extra careful upkeep'.[38] This became increasingly difficult for the Corporation to maintain especially given economic pressures from the 1970s onwards. High-rise blocks in particular also proved difficult and costly to maintain which had knock-on effects on the budget for landscaping areas surrounding the blocks. For high-rise residents in Castlemilk, their demands for improved and regular maintenance illustrated the severity of the problem and perhaps accounted for the fatalistic responses of some residents including Mr Cable who had moved to a high flat from a larger low rise property in Castlemilk and who suggested that 'all the schemes are the same'.[39]

Miracle in the Gorbals? City centre living

The Corporation's planners took a radically different approach in the Gorbals, as the city's first inner-city slum clearance Comprehensive Development Area (CDA). The plans received a good deal of attention in the architectural press in the UK and beyond. Ninian Johnstone, a prominent local architect, celebrated the 'Miracle in the Gorbals' describing the planned CDA as 'the largest of its kind so far attempted' and 'one which bids fair to make history'.[40] Most of the 111 acre site containing four-storey tenements was to be cleared as 87 per cent of the 7,605 dwellings had only one or two rooms, only 3 per cent had baths and only 22 per cent had internal toilets. Before clearance there were 394 occupied shops and 48 public houses in the area. It was expected that reconstruction would take 20 years. In the first stage, four integrated high-rise housing estates would be constructed. This was accompanied by a main shopping centre, medical clinic, cinema and services trades area which would be followed in stage two by schools, local shopping centres and a community centre. However, there were to be only 57 replacement shops and 9 pubs. There were significant delays in the central shopping centre and the cinema was never built.

Despite the reduction in the level of amenities residents in the Gorbals in the late 1960s were overwhelmingly positive about the estate given its close geographical proximity to the city centre, commenting on the 'handiness of the place' and the fact 'you can walk into town from here'. 'It is not like some schemes where you are miles from everybody' remarked Mrs Bennett.[41] It is important to note here that a significant proportion of Gorbals' residents had not been geographically relocated; former Gorbals' tenement residents moved a short distance to the new high-rise flats.[42] This was significant in terms of their sense of wellbeing and the maintenance of social networks. And the inner-city location seems to have compensated for the concrete brutalism of the architecture in the redeveloped Gorbals. In fact some residents praised the scheme as being 'nicely laid out' with a focus on the 'good amenities' in the area, in particular shops, although there were complaints about delays in construction.[43] 'We are lucky' recorded Mrs McCann. For her the redeveloped Gorbals was 'convenient in every way as 'we have shops all round the scheme'.[44] Indeed residents in the inner-city in this estate as with others such as Wyndford and Moss Heights were obviously fortunate that they were closer to the city centre or to established communities but more considered planning and provision of amenities also made the chores of everyday life easier. They also did not need to rely on an expensive and unreliable bus service.

'You've to go into the city': social life

Satisfaction with life in high-rise estates was not all about everyday necessities; the provision of places in which to socialise was also important to people. Glasgow Corporation was keen to discourage the proliferation of pubs and betting shops in the new estates constructed in the post-war decades in an attempt to positively influence working-class culture in line with the views of the Labour Governments of these years.[45] This was a deliberate strategy rather than omission in provision and harks back to attempts to encourage rational recreation that accompanied the 'respectable' and 'temperate' working class politics of the labour movement in the West of Scotland as opposed to the 'rough' pleasures enjoyed by the masses.[46] Notably the housing convenor David Gibson was a 'teetotaller' which was not uncommon in the ranks of the most ideological of the left-wing of the Labour Party in Glasgow. However, rather than ensuring that the city's infamous hard-drinking culture was transformed, instead men, and especially younger men, travelled further to go to pubs to meet their friends and frequent betting shops. In Castlemilk Mr Jackson, who stated that living in a peripheral estate 'doesn't bother me because I'm never here', nevertheless complained that 'By the time I'm home from work – fed and changed it's not worth going out'. He suggested that 'for a night's enjoyment you've to go into the city, there is no social life in the scheme at all'.[47] Living in a peripheral estate restricted his ability to be among his friends and enjoy himself. Likewise Mr Holt, who had grown up and 'belonged to' Castlemilk and was therefore used to it agreed that 'there's certainly not any entertainment which would save you going out to the town'.[48]

Indeed, those who had relocated from areas in the inner city tended to travel back to these areas in the evenings and weekends to socialise, mainly in public houses, maintaining a link with their 'old districts' and thus not fully committing to life in their new environment. In this sense, and for some men in particular, the peripheral estates remained dormitory settlements. The surroundings of the estate were insignificant as they spent so little time there. In fact the influx of men from the peripheral estates to the public houses that survived demolition in the Gorbals has become one of Glasgow's most prominent collective memories, captured in popular fiction and local histories.[49] Mr Brady who had relocated from the Gorbals described Castlemilk as 'fairly nice' but he was 'never in the scheme' as 'I go outside it for my amusement – drinks and so on. Well there's nothing in it – there's no public houses – no recreations – no halls – public halls – or not enough of them'.[50] Mrs McAdam who had moved from Linthouse in Govan in the inner city stated that she 'hated Castlemilk' because 'There's nothing for men here – except a bowling green for old men. My man likes a few pubs around and betting shops!'[51] Old habits died hard for some despite the Corporation's efforts to reform behaviour.

Until the late 1970s many public houses in working-class areas of Glasgow excluded women or relegated them to a separate room. Mrs Williamson recalled the segregation in pubs in the Wyndford estate:

> The men stood at the bar and the women at the lounge. I mean the likes of, what's called the "Botany" nowadays. That was a very, very manly pub. Very few – very, very few women ever went in and, eh.... Very, very strict pub.[52]

But there were few alternative social facilities for women on the estates and women did not have the same opportunity or freedom as their husbands to travel to the city centre and 'old districts' to see their friends. Mrs Bradley who had moved from Oatlands, an inner city area, 'quite liked it' in Castlemilk but felt 'we haven't got anything up here' and in particular 'there's not very much organised activity in the evening'.[53] Such was the shortage of social facilities that membership of the recently built community centre was full within the first week. Going out with their husbands was also expensive, especially paying for babysitters, bus fares and taxis. Interestingly men did not seem to have the same concerns over the cost of travel to socialise. Mrs Green suggested this would have been a bit cheaper if there was a pub in Castlemilk.[54] Instead there were only two cafes.[55] Mrs Black, a widow, even suggested that a hall could be constructed where the 'young mothers could dance in and meet at night' as 'they're very lonely'.[56] There were certainly fewer options for women to leave the estate for entertainment in the evening and no cosy pubs, restaurants or halls for the women who lived in high flats to meet. John, who grew up in Castlemilk and returned to live in a high flat with his wife Carol in 1969 when they were both 22 years old, reflected with regret that after they married he:

> was pretty irresponsible like most guys of my generation and age ... I was probably married about ten years before I realised I was actually married, you know, before it dawned on me. I just carried on as if I was a single guy with the rest of my pals ... Carol talked about going out with the kids, but she was the one who done the most of that ... it was partly the culture of the time, like it or not.[57]

However, not all men struggled to settle in high-rise estates and did not feel the need to maintain old routines in the inner city or city centre. Tricia, who moved to Castlemilk as a child in the 1960s, described her father establishing an active social life in Castlemilk, initially by joining the local Labour club when a young married man, then later the bowling club. Some of his friends remained men he had known in the Gorbals as well as work colleagues that lived in the high-rise blocks. Clearly some men were ready for a change and embraced life in the peripheral estates by finding ways to introduce and perhaps adapt their version of working class masculine social culture, as well as pursuing new hobbies:

> ... he'd joined the Labour club, not for the politics of course, but he would [laughs] he'd worked in the GPO [General Post Office] an' a lot of the people he met there, like three or four o' them lived up the flats. Ah don't know, ah, it was just a coincidence. An' plus he'd known them from the Gorbals years ago, from the 'sooth side' as my

dad would say. Em, an' my dad, he joined there an' he had a fantastic social life in there, but they were there Friday, Saturday, Sunday. An' it was a new club an' my dad seemed to be popular there and they were there all the time. And by that time I was old enough to watch Lorna an' they were, they were there all, every weekend. An' then they opened a bowling club in Dougrie an' he moved tae that an' he did exceptionally well with the bowls. He won a lot of championships an' so they began in the bowling club, they would go there at the weekends, eh, an' that wis his friends. An' they enjoyed that, well ah don't think my mum so much but she went along, but my dad absolutely loved it.[58]

The meagre provision of amenities and services in Castlemilk relative to the size of the population and the fact that the vast majority of high-rise residents had moved there from another part of the city contributed to feelings of isolation. The peripheral location of Castlemilk was further compounded by the isolated nature of the high-rise blocks within the estate. The obstacles to community-making were thus manifold, something that was far less evident in the Gorbals as in other estates closer to the city where, despite the objectively alienating concrete environment, people were able to retain existing social contacts and make new ones on account of the far greater opportunities for casual interactions on and around the estate. Moss Heights for instance, which was relatively close to the city and adjacent to a range of amenities in Cardonald was described by Mr Welch as 'a vertical village':

> I mean the Moss Heights was a village at that time, I suppose it's a bit of a cliché, but it was a vertical village. And like a traditional village, if you lived in the one close with people you would have quite close relationships with them. You'd know, quite well, families and people in adjacent closes, and even people from the other block, you would know quite well.[59]

In Castlemilk on the other hand, the layout of and level of provision on the estate was identified as an issue from its inception, quickly leading to isolation (particularly amongst women and the elderly), and by the 1980s requiring 'comprehensive regeneration' to tackle the 'deep-rooted nature of deprivation'.[60]

It is significant that levels of satisfaction in the Gorbals exceeded those on peripheral estates. The concrete-scape of the redeveloped Gorbals does not seem to have concerned residents beyond the brutalist appearance of the blocks and here there were fewer comments on the shared outdoor spaces requiring maintenance than in peripheral locations, although the blocks were about the same age. It would appear that the geographical location and distance from the city centre, as well as the level of amenities provided made all the difference to residents' satisfaction. The one exception was the lack of designated space for use by children which featured prominently in residents' responses in the 1960s on all estates and which might be regarded as symptomatic of a general failure by planners to pay sufficient attention to the outside environment of the high-rise estate which played such a significant role in facilitating sociability and communality, especially amongst women.

Children and play: 'nae use for the bairns'

Not everyone perceived high-rise estates as unsuitable for children. In contrast with the housing conditions many had left, some could see the benefits of the open spaces and fresh air, particularly on the peripheral estates. Mr Smith, who had a three year old son, suggested that the location of high blocks in Castlemilk on the edge of the hills known as the Cathkin Braes was 'healthy for the kids'.[61] Mr Harold, a father of three, agreed that 'it's also built in a good place for the kids – they have all the hills to play in'.[62] John even persuaded his parents to move from low rise flats in Castlemilk in 1981 to live in the high-rise blocks when he was 12 years old as he had friends who lived there and loved the freedom they had:

> As I say I was going about with those boys and I really loved the flats when we moved up there it was absolutely brilliant I am not kidding you it was like coming from the city … and moving to the country. People were collecting eggs, ferrets and greyhounds and lurchers and going hunting, air rifles and fishing and all that … it was like night and day…. You came out your house and you were near enough there you just came up the back and you were near enough on the Braes. Many a time we spent up there – brilliant.[63]

Such freedom was also important for parents in the late 1960s, especially those that wanted better for their children than growing up in an inner-city tenement. As a mother of two sons, suggested, 'I was brought up in a back court [shared space behind tenement blocks] and it didn't do me any harm, but we want something better for our kids'. She liked living in the multi-storeys in Castlemilk as 'there's plenty of room for them to play – there's grassy slopes at the back or plenty of room around the block. They get good freedom'.[64] Mrs Cook who had an eight-year-old daughter agreed that 'there are plenty of fields and open spaces, in fact, here there's everything that anyone can wish for'.[65] Such sentiments are reminiscent of views expressed by the residents of the new towns: fresh air and space to play for the next generation were always seen as significant benefits of moving out of the city.[66]

Yet there were few formal play spaces and facilities provided for play in either peripheral or city locations despite the fact that since the 1950s the government had been concerned about the social consequences of children living in flats, commissioning research on children's play, especially in new housing estates, including those with high-rise blocks.[67] The necessity of play became increasingly central to notions of child development in the immediate post-war decades.[68] Pearl Jephcott not only paid a great deal of attention to children in the high flats study but she was subsequently commissioned to conduct a study in a high-rise estate in Birmingham on the effects of living high on children.[69] The main fear, which gained currency, not only amongst academic researchers but also in popular circles including parents, was that 'living high' resulted in children being 'hemmed in', restricting their ability to engage in outdoor, uninhibited and social play, which in turn would have a long-term negative impact on their social and educational development.[70] Parents recognised that their children suffered from not mixing with other children of their own age – few in the study had friends on the same floor – and from being cooped up indoors with one mother commenting: 'Makes the children wild when they go out because of the restraint at home – they go mad.'[71] Jephcott described high-rise flats as 'nae use for the bairns' and 'somehow alien to the children' with Lady Allen of Hurtwood regarding the Red Road flats as 'a kind of psychological pollution' where 'a lift hall is their only playground'.[72] Mrs Stewart's concerns about her own three children under the age of five who appeared less 'advanced' than children of relatives, provided Jephcott with the justification she needed to conduct a comparison between primary school children living in high and low rise in the city.[73] The small study conducted by one of Jephcott's students, found no evidence to support the notion that living high had a deleterious impact on those children's academic attainment and social development although it did reveal the constraints on children expressing themselves through play, both inside and outside: children were 'stopped playing where they wish and forbidden to enjoy themselves in the noisy manner common to children of their age'.[74]

The study did reveal the lack of dedicated play areas. Given the shortage of space inside the flats and fears of children accessing dangerous verandas and lifts, parents were understandably desirous of outdoor space equipped for children and preferably supervised by adults. Yet, in practical terms, going outside to play was more difficult for young children living in high flats because of the need to use the lift or stairs on their own, and in more traditional housing children could be observed far more easily.[75] Parents were not able to 'glance now and then' to see if their child was all right as 'the child can slip under the block, round the corner and vanish from sight'.[76] Such difficulties associated with allowing children outside to play were set to verse in the well-known 'Jeely Piece Song' composed in 1967 which refers to the tradition of mothers throwing a sandwich (known as a piece) out of a tenement window to the children below, a practice made more difficult by the height of the towers:

> I'm a skyscraper wean [child], I live on the nineteenth flair,
> But I'm no gaun oot to play ony mair,
> Since we moved to Castlemilk, I'm wasting away,
> 'Cause I'm getting one less meal every day.
>
> O ye cannae fling pieces oot a twenty-story flat,
> Seven-hundred hungry weans will testify to that,
> If it's butter, cheese or jeely, if the breid is plain or pan,
> The odds against it reaching earth are ninety-nine to one.[77]

The obstacles to safe play outdoors were compounded in the late 1960s by a lack of dedicated play facilities near the blocks. High-rise towers in the UK were surrounded by empty spaces in order to meet the building regulations relating to access to daylight.[78] In Castlemilk all the high and low rise blocks of flats were surrounded by open expanses of grassland which was undesignated but definitely not to be used for children's play. 'No ball games' signs were common on most of Glasgow's housing estates in an effort to maintain standards and the grass being ruined by football and other boisterous activities. In addition, the grassed areas around high-rise blocks were particularly difficult for residents to take ownership of and use in contrast with low rise flats which tended to have space in a communal garden where children could play. Around the high flats in Castlemilk however, Jephcott's researchers found that there was 'hardly any casual grass at all' for children to play on and 'no children's playground'. Older children had to cross a main road with no zebra crossing and younger children had to be accompanied by their parents to access suitable play areas.

In the inner city Gorbals there was 'no play equipment or amenity area' within the estate although there was a large grass area and Queen Elizabeth Square theoretically had significant 'amenity space' under the blocks as it was built on pilotis or concrete columns.[79] The architect had envisaged that this underneath space would provide the 'street life' of the tenements. In reality it frequently became a wind tunnel and was largely a transitory space rather than somewhere people would linger. There was a large playground with swings and a roundabout across the nearby main road but no pedestrian crossing for the children. A climbing frame was situated in a concrete piazza, illustrated in Figure 3.3. Preschool children therefore played on their balconies, those aged 6–10 were able to cross the road to the playground and the children over 11 also played here and went further afield to nearby public parks including Glasgow Green.

Safety and delinquency

The lack of designated play space for children of all ages caused parents to express concerns about safety, children's development and delinquency, fears that were in line with broader social anxieties emerging in this period about children's freedom.[80] While street play and considerable freedom to roam were still features of quite young children's lives in Britain until the 1970s, parents in high-rise estates had very particular worries about letting children out to play on their own. The concern was that 'where the parents were unusually nervous about safety or unusually keen to raise the children's standards of behaviour' children would be kept cooped up indoors.[81] A father of three children under five years old in Castlemilk, stated that:

Figure 3.3 Children's playground in Hutchesontown in the Gorbals.

our wee lassie of four can't get out because they can't use the lift and they can't be left out to play on their own. You'd worry about them out there on their own. They always have to be taken out.[82]

In the Gorbals road safety was one cause of concern. A father of two older children felt that the only nearby swing park was too far away across a road that was 'very busy with traffic' and 'dangerous for children to cross'.[83]

The absence of responsible adults to supervise children raised fears that if there was an incident they would be too far away to intervene. A mother of two would have preferred a house with a 'back and front door and a garden for the sake of the kiddies'.[84] Some residents suggested, not only that a playground be installed near the block, but that this be a space where 'someone could keep an eye on them'. Supervised playgrounds were supported by experts in the field of children's play in the 1960s but were rarely funded by municipal authorities.[85] Play pens, which were essentially fenced in grassed areas, were a solution to keeping younger children safe and had been included in other estates in Glasgow but not in Castlemilk. Even then children could not be left unattended and mothers either sat on benches installed by the Corporation, on walls or brought down their own chairs to watch their children play.[86]

Despite parents expressing worries about their children's access to outdoor play, older children did escape the flats. One summer evening in the late 1960s, University of Glasgow researchers counted in five minutes around 120 children around the Red Road estate and just 17 adults. A similar count in Castlemilk identified 90 children and 'not even half a dozen adults'.[87] For some residents the lack of adult supervision, few play facilities and boredom could result in so many children becoming 'a law unto themselves', with destruction, vandalism and noisy playing being the main concerns. In Castlemilk one resident complained that 'there's too many kids about the entrance'.[88] Similarly Mrs Mills suggested that 'a good playground for the kids ... would take them away from the blocks'. She felt that 'there wouldn't be so much damage done to the blocks if they could go to a playground'.[89] Planners had argued that 'juvenile delinquency would be expected to diminish with the substitution of good homes for the present unsatisfactory ones'.[90] In reality far more was required than simply good housing. Residents explicitly linked vandalism around the blocks and in the estate with boredom and suggested that teenagers 'need a dance hall and a cinema to keep them off the streets. They're just like animals they're allowed to roam the streets because there are no facilities to keep them in the scheme'.[91] Mrs Gardner also suggested that the 'young ones' were 'making a slum of the place!' and she blamed their parents for letting them 'run wild' as 'they can't keep an eye on them'.[92] Complaints also extended to the green spaces in the scheme with Mr Kerr angry that the Corporation's efforts to 'lay out the ground' was 'getting no peace from the young people' who 'pull and run through the young trees and won't allow anything to grow'.[93]

The preoccupation of many residents, however, was the need to provide facilities for older boys to prevent vandalism. The football kickabout near the high-rise blocks in Castlemilk was dominated by teenage boys. As a mother of three, stated 'There is a football park but the big ones won't let the younger ones in – they punch them'.[94] Meanwhile those with younger sons suggested that there should be even more provision for boys who 'seem to be kind of lost looking' as 'they don't have much to do' and 'could do with a sports club'. Mrs Muir, who had a four-year-old son also suggested that 'we could do with boys brigade and scouts here'.[95] So even where the only provision made for children's play in the late 1960s was aimed at boys, there was a perception that more could be done to keep boys occupied and out of trouble. Gang violence in the peripheral estates in Glasgow in the 1960s was the subject of significant social comment and concern.[96] Boys, it was thought, had a 'reputation for physical violence' as tenement life ensured that 'to survive he must learn to be tough and aggressive'.[97] If this was the case in four-storey tenements then in high rise, where boys had even more distance from the supervision of their parents, there were greater fears. As well as concerns over destructive behaviour and vandalism, it was perhaps hoped that providing facilities for physical activity would also help boys avoid gang culture when they were older. Few noticed that there was no equivalent provision for girls though Jephcott did observe that 'no one seemed to have thought about girls' needs as regards their type of play'.[98]

One solution to the issue of children's play proposed by parents and researchers was the provision of facilities for young children inside the blocks although motivations were not necessarily in harmony. Jephcott's team had collaborated with the Scottish Pre-School Playgroups Association to support mothers in running a voluntary playgroup in a high-rise block in Royston to encourage constructive play with their young children. The initiative failed. The mothers required supervised childcare which would allow them to work. As Mrs Devine, a mother of three, suggested the Corporation should provide nurseries for younger children in or near the high-rise blocks as 'the rents were going up' and 'some of the mothers could take a part-time job'.[99] The playgroup model, on the other hand, was reliant on mothers' unpaid voluntary work on a regular basis and a degree of engagement which these working-class women were unable to give.[100] While the nature of the housing was not the sole reason for the failure of the playgroup experiment, when the Scottish Pre-School Playgroup Association engaged with 'deprived communities' in Glasgow in the 1970s, high-rise estates were seen as particularly in need of playgroup provision but it was recognised that often the needs of the mothers were greater than those of the children: 'Mothers have a need to come and be calmed down'.[101] Lack of play and care provision for children on these estates was a contributory factor in women in particular experiencing isolation and poor mental health.[102] According to Hilda Brown, a student who conducted research on mothers' isolation as part of Jephcott's project:

[The] reasons for being housebound are the same for both women in high blocks and low rise housing. However mothers in high blocks have an added difficulty in waiting for lifts, manoeuvring prams into them, and the old problem of difficulties of children's play. Therefore all these factors make a difference to the frequency with which they go out, and their dissatisfaction or frustration at being isolated since if the children are always in the flat, they must become rather annoying at times.[103]

In this case the relationship between relocation, often away from support networks, and the unique character of high-rise housing was critical to the emergence, or not, of communality. The absence, on some estates, of places where mothers of young children might meet such as mother and baby clinics, playgroups and playparks served to limit the possibilities for casual contact which really only occurred in the lifts and laundry areas inside the blocks. For high-rise housing to succeed for its residents, far more was required than a modern flat. The amenities and services on the estate were necessary to ameliorate the danger of domestic privacy turning into domestic imprisonment. Lorraine and Tricia described the turning point for their mother when her flat in Castlemilk was broken into sometime in the 1980s. Her door was broken down despite the security of three locks and 'that jist devastated her ...'. Her suspicion was that the perpetrators must have been tipped off by her neighbours and lived on the estate themselves.[104] She 'never recovered' from the experience as 'she knew that it was this crowd and she felt they were all laughing at her all the time. It just freaked her out completely.... From then on it was ma mother's mission tae get out o' there.'[105]

Places to play

A very different perspective in high-rise estates emerges when former residents recall their childhoods. While adults were often fearful and anxious for their children, an anxiety that only grew as gangs and drugs became serious issues, those who recall their childhoods on the high-rise estates emphasise the freedom and ingenuity in finding places to play. The only formal provision for play near the high-rise blocks in the Gorbals in the late 1960s was the play park across a main road. Catherine, whose family moved into the block in 1965 when she was a baby, remembered this park fondly:

> The big giant chute, that was about thirty feet high! … Ye'd slide nearly on tae the bloody wall of the church…. Em, called it the animal park because it, ah don't know what made them, who put theym in but it wis like cows an' sheeps an' aw that an'. We hid a big chute an' the big swings an' the roundabout, it wis excellent.[106]

However the lack of play spaces meant this park was very overcrowded, which ensured that as children got older they found their own spaces to play around the blocks. Paul, who moved with his family into the block in 1966, spoke about exploring beyond this formal space:

> There was this, I suppose like Council Nursery shed which was quite big but they had these big doors onto it. Childish curiosity would always get the better of you so you grew up watching your peers and all the rest of them trying to get in there. So when you grew up to be about eight that's what you did. What that was taking you into was just over the fence of this safe swing park area … but there was lots of like greenery around this shed and I suppose this is when I started thinking I am too big for the swings now so we started to explore. So we explored that area.[107]

Older children would also venture further afield to another play area in the Gorbals referred to as 'the jumps'. As Kozlowsky argues, the architectural profession began to give more thought to the design of children's play-grounds to take account of changing attitudes to child development and the importance of play.[108] At 'the jumps', the precursor of later adventure playgrounds children, both boys and girls, could jump off the big log or climb to the top of the frame thereby taking risks and challenging them-selves through play, which was a major preoccupation of play experts in the 1960s.[109] Paul's testimony supports these assertions about the import-ance of what he describes as creating 'a sense of bravado':

> Play time was so adventurous because they had spent time developing what we called the jumps which was the same area but just off to the

left and that's when Glasgow discovered Parkour! Big time! These kids that bang on about Parkour – forget it! You know I saw some amazing stuff down there, excellent stuff.... I don't know who designed that area but they had the right idea. I mean seriously thinking about that play area alone we all became acrobats. Big-time. I always thought to myself whoever designed this did it well you know. It was designed to create a sense of bravado within you – you know. Go on – do it – do it – jump it – and you did.[110]

As a girl, Catherine was theoretically more restricted. Her mother had far more rules about where she was allowed to play: 'Oh aye, we were just allowed tae play in the scheme. We were not, wurnae allowed out there'. She was permitted to go to the play park across the road from the block but not just 'go exploring' like Paul. She did not go to 'the jumps' either mainly because of her mother's fears of traffic and perhaps of wanting her children to stay close by: '... you had tae cross about three roads, busy roads, an' no way. An' we did sneak sometimes, an' ah says, if we get caught we're gonnae get killed'. But Catherine did defy her mum stating 'But eh, we never got caught'.[111]

Children were also inventive in their play in the amenity space under and around the blocks. There was risky behaviour here too. Paul describes the games that he and his friends used to play under the block:

What we did was we would run up the big concrete feet of the flat. That's what we did or play underneath the flats. Then play wind catcher. So you would get your jacket up and out and literally do a Dorothy [Wizard of Oz] and literally get taken off your feet because the wind was crazy.[112]

High-rise residents in the late 1960s believed that the absence of formal provision of play facilities restricted children's ability to play.[113] Yet on the whole, oral history testimonies of former residents who grew up in high flats in these estates contradict this view. While historian Thomson has emphasised the 'loss of freedom' for children in this period, there is little evidence of this in our narratives.[114] Parents, as we have seen, were concerned with safety, but retrospective narratives produced in the 2010s emphasise children's agency through play, imagination and adaptability. Children subverted the intentions of the architect in the outdoor spaces round the blocks just as their parents did in the modification of the interiors of their homes. In the Gorbals, Spence probably did not envisage children climbing up the pilotis or playing 'wind catcher' under the high-rise blocks.[115] And Tricia who described playing in woods and in the street around her block in Castlemilk, was able to contradict the lyrics of the much loved Jeely Piece song: 'ah used tae shout up at ma mum … awright a piece an' jam an' that's whit wid come oot … I used tae stand at the bottom an' she wid be throwin them oot the eighth storey …'.[116]

Conclusions

Perceptions of 'planning failure' are prominent in popular memory in Glasgow in relation to both high-rise estates in the inner city but more especially on the peripheral estates. This chapter has prioritised the lived experiences of former residents rather than repeating clichés focusing on neglected concrete-scapes or windswept barren greenspaces. Nevertheless, there was some truth in these stereotypical representations of multi-storey estates. Design and planning of outdoor space did and does matter, affecting not only people's experience of negotiating everyday tasks such as shopping, walking to school and engaging in leisure activities but also influencing residents' perceptions of the area more generally.

Examination of two very different estates has demonstrated how design of the estate beyond the block had different outcomes. In the inner-city area of the Gorbals, which had been comprehensively planned and designed, residents were generally satisfied with their concrete surroundings, at least when the estate was only a few years old, largely as a result of their proximity to the city centre and the provision of amenities. On the periphery of the city in Castlemilk, on the other hand, high-rise residents perceived there to have been oversights by planners, both in terms of amenity provision, but also in the expanses of undesignated greenspace that predominated on the estate and around the high-rise blocks. Glasgow's peripheral estates, characterised as 'barracks' or 'dormitory settlements' where planners focused on housing first, were isolated geographically from the city centre and residents had to travel to undertake all the basic functions of everyday life: to go to work, to perform everyday chores such as shopping and to socialise. For many this sense of distance from the city centre far outweighed the benefits of the location, especially in winter. And men and women experienced the estate differently. Mothers of young children struggled with inadequate pathways, shops a 20-minute walk away and an absence of safe play facilities. Men who were out at work all day were far less concerned with these everyday challenges, were more likely to have access to a car and could escape the estate for their leisure. Living in the block itself was not the problem. As discussed in Chapter 2, the high-rise flat could provide the material environment and domestic privacy many wished for but the failure of the Corporation to plan for and provide amenities and the absence of a fully integrated and affordable transport infrastructure caused residents major problems, especially women and older adults. Yet while adults fretted about their children's social development and safety and consistently complained of the absence of play facilities, children themselves experienced freedom, despite the existence of street gangs on many estates, and recall, albeit often through rose-tinted spectacles, opportunities for imaginative and creative play.

This chapter has identified how the outside was as important as the inside for those who were relocated to high-rise estates. People's enjoyment of their modern flat was compromised by the symbolic violence of the estate. Over time the failure to invest in basic maintenance and security meant that the flats that people appreciated became a refuge from the estate and in some cases a prison. While this was not the case on every high-rise estate in the city, where decline did occur, the concern with reputation became increasingly important to residents in the context of deindustrialisation and the residualisation of council housing. By the 1980s the high-rise flats in the Gorbals had become emblematic of urban deprivation in the city. This coincided with national criticisms of high rise as a solution to slum clearance where this housing form effectively became a signifier of 'blight' in the British inner city and a focus of policy intervention to re-establish 'community', the focus of Chapter 4.

Notes

1 Ade Kearns, Oliver Kearns, and Louise Lawson, 'Notorious places: image, reputation, stigma: the role of newspapers in area reputations for social housing estates', *Housing Studies*, 28:5 (2013), pp. 579–98.

2 This was certainly the view of Jephcott and was subsequently echoed in subsequent studies such as Coleman in *Utopia on Trial*.

3 M. Willis (Ministry of Housing and Local Government), *Living in Flats* (London, HMSO, 1952); Ministry of Housing and Local Government, *Homes for Today and Tomorrow*; Vere Hole (Ministry of Technology, Building Research Station), *Children's Play on Housing Estates* (London, HMSO, 1966); Scottish Housing Advisory Committee, *Housing Management in Scotland* (Edinburgh, HMSO, 1967).

4 This ranged from architectural criticism such as Nikolaus Pevsner's Reith Lectures of 1955 entitled 'The Englishness of English Art: Architecture and Planning: The Functional Approach' (see www.bbc.co.uk/sounds/play/p00hg1b0) to left-wing critiques such as *New Society*'s special issue entitled 'The concrete Jerusalem: the failure of the clean sweep' Vol. 38, Iss. 742 (Dec 23, 1976): i–xvi; and finally accounts of peoples' experiences of living on modernist estates featured in the tabloids and on television, for example National Library of Scotland, Moving Image Archive: 'Gorbals old Gorbals new – One woman's story', 1966 (2471) https://movingimage.nls.uk/film/2471.

5 M. Burbridge, *High Density Housing: a Social Perspective* (MHLG, London, 1969); Ministry of Housing and Local Government, *Families Living at High Density* (London, 1970); Department of the Environment (UK), *The Estate Outside the Dwelling: Reactions of Residents to Aspects of Housing Layout'* (HMSO, London, 1972), p. 3; B. Abrams, and J. Conway, *The Social Effects of Living Off the Ground* (Department of the Environment, London, DOE Information Paper No. 9, 1975); F.D. Becker, 'The effect of physical and social factors on residents' sense of security in multi-family housing developments', *Journal of Architectural Research*, 4 (1975), pp. 18–24.

6 R. Forrest and A. Murie, 'Residualization and council housing: Aspects of the changing social relations of housing tenure', *Journal of Social Policy* 12:4 (1983), pp. 453–68.

7 Michael Pacione, *Glasgow: the Socio-spatial Development of the City* (Oxford, 1995). See also S. Watt, 'Metamorphosis in the Gorbals' *The New Yorker*, 24 October 1959, p. 137.

8 Miles Glendinning interview with Tom Smyth, former principal architect, Scottish Division, Wimpey Ltd, 5 July 1987. See Diane Watters, *Home Builders, Mactaggart and Mickel and the Scottish Housebuilding Industry* (RCAHMS, Edinburgh, 1999), p. 290.

9 UGA, DC127/1/1-10/1, Castlemilk.

10 Jephcott, *Homes in High Flats*, p. 66 and Appendix D, pp. 157–8.

11 UGA, DC127/1/1-10/1: Gorbals.

12 R. Brown, 'Glasgow demands action on crime', *Guardian*, 28 Mar 1968, p. 20; H. Jackson, 'Out of the dumps' *Guardian*, 23 Oct 1968, p. 9; W.S. Churchill, 'Society's failure to invest enough in housing' *The Times*, 21 Oct 1969, p. 11; S. Cornwall, 'Fading past of Glasgow', *Guardian*, 26 May 1970, p. 16, R. Sharpe, 'Overspill plan still has a long way to go' *The Times*, 6 June 1970, p. II. N.A. Sims, 'Letters to the editor: Easterhouse: Glasgow's shame', *Guardian*, 31 Aug 1970, p. 8.

13 Interview with Lorraine (Castlemilk, b. 1964), 2015.

14 Interview with Brian (Gorbals, b. *c.*1960). 2015.

15 Glendinning and Muthesius, *Tower Block*, pp. 220–46.

16 Castlemilk History, *The Big Flit: Castlemilk's First Tenants* (Castlemilk, 1990). On the supermarket campaign see www.bbc.co.uk/news/uk-scotland-glasgow-west-48749338 (accessed 25.11.2019).

17 www.heraldscotland.com/news/12250485.billy-connolly-classically-described-the-new-estates-as-deserts-wi-windaes/ (accessed 25.11.2019).

18 National Library of Scotland, Moving Image Archive: 'Social Problems', 1965 (4203).

19 UGA, DC 127/11: V. Somerville, 'Castlemilk Flats', October 1967.

20 Jephcott, *Homes in High Flats*, p. 66.

21 UGA, DC127/1/1-10/1, Castlemilk.

22 UGA, DC127/1/1-10/1, Castlemilk.

23 UGA, DC127/1/1-10/1, Castlemilk.

24 UGA, DC127/1/1-10/1, Castlemilk.

25 UGA, DC127/1/1-10/1, Castlemilk.

26 UGA, DC127/1/1-10/1, Castlemilk.

27 UGA, DC127/1/1-10/1, Castlemilk.

28 UGA, DC127/1/1-10/1, 4 respondents, Castlemilk.

29 UGA, DC127/1/1-10/1, Castlemilk; Jephcott, *Homes in High Flats*, p. 67.

30 UGA, DC127/1/1-10/1, Castlemilk.
31 Jephcott, *Homes in High Flats*, pp. 65–9.
32 UGA, DC127/1/1-10/1, Castlemilk.
33 Interview with Tricia (Castlemilk, b.1957), 2015.
34 Jephcott, *Homes in High Flats*, p. 59
35 Lawrence, *Me, Me, Me?* p. 52.
36 Jephcott, *Homes in High Flats*, pp. 59–60.
37 UGA, DC127/1/1-10/1, Castlemilk.
38 Jephcott, *Homes in High Flats*, p. 61.
39 UGA, DC127/1/1-10/1, Castlemilk.
40 N. Johnston, 'Miracle in the Gorbals?', *Architectural Prospect*, Spring 1957.
41 UGA, DC127/1/1-10/1, Gorbals.
42 Ade Kearns, Valerie Wright, Lynn Abrams, Barry Hazley, 'Slum clearance and relocation: a reassessment of social outcomes combining short-term and long-term perspectives', *Housing Studies*, 34:2 (2019), pp. 201–25.
43 UGA, DC127/1/1-10/1, Gorbals.
44 UGA, DC127/1/1-10/1, Gorbals.
45 Alistair Fair, *Modern Playhouses: An Architectural History of Britain's New Theatres, 1945–1985* (Oxford University Press, Oxford, 2018); Damer, *Scheming*.
46 See Tanya Cheadle, 'Music hall, "mashers" and the "unco guid": competing masculinities in Victorian Glasgow' in Lynn Abrams and Elizabeth Ewan (eds), *Nine Centuries of Man: Manhood and Masculinities in Scottish History* (Edinburgh University Press, Edinburgh, 2016), pp. 223–41; Callum G. Brown, 'Popular Culture and the Continuing Struggle for Rational Recreation' in T.M. Devine and R.J. Finlay (eds) *Scotland in the Twentieth Century* (Edinburgh University Press, Edinburgh, 1996); T.C. Smout, *A Century of the Scottish People, 1830–1950* (Collins, London, 1986) pp. 133–58. See *Evening Times*, 29 October 1953.
47 UGA, DC127/1/1-10/1: Castlemilk.
48 UGA, DC127/1/1-10/1: Castlemilk.
49 Jeff Torrington, *Swing Hammer Swing* (Minerva, London, 1993). D. Gill, *Gorbals and Oatlands* (PublishNation, 22 June 2015). See also www.oldglasgowpubs.co.uk/cornergorbals.html (accessed 10.12.2019).
50 UGA, DC127/1/1-10/1, Castlemilk.
51 UGA, DC127/1/1-10/1, Castlemilk.
52 Interview with Mrs Betty Williamson (Wyndford, b.1949), 2015.
53 UGA, DC127/1/1-10/1, Castlemilk.
54 UGA, DC127/1/1-10/1, Castlemilk.
55 Jephcott, *Homes in High Flats*, p. 66.
56 UGA, DC127/1/1-10/1, Castlemilk.
57 Interview with John and Carol (Castlemilk, b.1947), 2015.
58 Interview with Tricia (Castlemilk, b.1957), 2015.
59 Interview with Mr Leslie Welch (Moss Heights, b.1950), 2015.
60 Kearns *et al.*, 'Slum clearance', p. 209.
61 UGA, DC127/1/1-10/1, Castlemilk.
62 UGA, DC127/1/1-10/1, Castlemilk.
63 Interview with John, 2015 (Castlemilk, b.1969), 2015.
64 UGA, DC127/1/1-10/1, Castlemilk.
65 UGA, DC127/1/1-10/1, Castlemilk.

66 Lynn Abrams, Barry Hazley, Valerie Wright, Ade Kearns, 'Aspiration, agency and the production of new selves in a Scottish new town, *c.*1947–*c.*2016', *Twentieth Century British History* 29:4 (2018), pp. 576–604.

67 For an overview see Valerie Wright, Ade Kearns, Lynn Abrams and Barry Hazley, 'Planning for Play: Seventy years of ineffective public policy? The example of Glasgow, Scotland', *Planning Perspectives* 34:2 (2019), pp. 243–63. See also Sub-Committee of the Central Housing Advisory Committee on Social Needs and Problems of Families Living in Large Blocks of Flats, *Living in Flats* (HMSO, London, 1952), Ministry of Housing and Local Government, *Homes for Today and Tomorrow*, para 176; Maizels, *Two to Five in High Flats*; Hole *Children's Play on Housing Estates.*

68 This was reflective of the growing acceptance and popularity of discourses concerning child welfare such as the work of John Bowlby and others who emphasised the importance of early childhood in 'determining the life chances of the adult'. Angela Davis, *Pre-school Childcare in England, 1939–2010* (Manchester University Press, Manchester, 2015).

69 P. Jephcott, *Young Families in High Flats* (Birmingham, 1975).

70 Lady Allen of Hurtwood, *Planning for Play* (Thames and Hudson, London, 1968), p. 14.

71 UGA, DC 127/16/1: J. Holland, 'A Comparison between Primary School Children living in Multi-Storey Housing, and those Living in Low-level Housing', p. 9.

72 Jephcott, *Homes in High Flats*, p. 49 and p. 80; Allen of Hurtwood, *Planning for Play*, pp. 14–15.

73 UGA, DC127/1/1-10/1, Castlemilk.

74 Jephcott, *Homes in High Flats*, p. 83; UGA, DC 127 16/1: Holland, 'A Comparison between Primary School Children', p. 47.

75 Jephcott, *Homes in High Flats*, p. 87.

76 Jephcott, *Homes in High Flats*, p. 87.

77 The Jeely Piece song was composed by Adam MacNaughton in 1967. See www.youtube.com/watch?v=8A7SAPmcwXA (accessed 10.12.2019).

78 Glendinning and Muthesius, *Tower Block*, pp. 35–52, 226 and 308.

79 Basil Spence was inspired by Le Corbusier's Unité d'Habitation which employed pilotis, a set of posts raising a building up from the ground. See www.fondationlecorbusier.fr and https://canmore.org.uk/site/70581/glasgow-hutchesontown-gorbals (accessed 10.12.2019).

80 See Matthew Thomson, *Lost Freedom. The Landscape of the Child and the British Post-war Settlement* (Oxford University Press, Oxford, 2013), pp. 133–52.

81 Jephcott, *Homes in High* Flats, p. 87.

82 UGA, DC127/1/1-10/1, Castlemilk.

83 UGA, DC127/1/1-10/1, Gorbals.

84 UGA, DC127/1/1-10/1, Castlemilk.

85 Hurtwood, *Planning for Play*; Wright *et al.*, 'Planning for Play', pp. 243–63, Jephcott, *Homes in High Flats*, pp. 141–2.

86 UGA, DC127/1/1-10/1, Castlemilk.

87 Jephcott, *Homes in High Flats*, p. 87.

88 UGA, DC127/1/1-10/1, Castlemilk.

89 UGA, DC127/1/1-10/1, Castlemilk.

90 Bruce, *First Planning Report*, p. 60.

91 UGA, DC127/1/1-10/1, Castlemilk.
92 UGA, DC127/1/1-10/1, Castlemilk.
93 UGA, DC127/1/1-10/1, Castlemilk.
94 UGA, DC127/1/1-10/1, Castlemilk.
95 UGA, DC127/1/1-10/1, Castlemilk.
96 Angela Bartie, 'Moral panics and Glasgow gangs: exploring "the New Wave of Glasgow Hooliganism", 1965–1970', *Contemporary British History* 24:3 (2010), pp. 385–408.
97 Jephcott, *Homes in High Flats*, pp. 87–8.
98 UGA, DC127/1/1-10/1, Castlemilk. Jephcott, *Homes in High Flats*, pp. 90–1.
99 UGA, DC127/1/1-10/1, Castlemilk.
100 Hazley *et al.*, 'People and their homes', pp. 728–45.
101 Institute of Education Archives: PLA/PPA/2/28: 'Playgroups in Areas of Need', 1977.
102 Lynn Abrams, Linda Fleming, Barry Hazley, Valerie Wright, Ade Kearns, 'Isolated and dependent: women and children in post-war social housing in Glasgow', *Women's History Review* 28:5 (2019), pp. 794–813.
103 UGA, DC127/15/4: Dissertation by Hilda Brown (1967).
104 Interview with Lorraine (Castlemilk, b.1964), 2015.
105 Interview with Tricia (Castlemilk, b.1957), 2015.
106 Interview with Catherine (Gorbals, b.1964), 2015.
107 Interview with Paul (Gorbals, b.1966), 2015.
108 Roy Kozlowsky, *The Architectures of Childhood: Children, Modern Architecture and Reconstruction in Postwar England* (Routledge, London, 2016).
109 Hurtwood, *Planning for Play*.
110 Interview with Paul (Gorbals, b.1966), 2015.
111 Interview with Catherine (Gorbals, b.1964), 2015.
112 Interview with Paul (Gorbals, b.1966), 2015.
113 Wright *et al.*, 'Planning for Play'.
114 Thomson, *Lost Freedom*, pp. 142–51.
115 B. Spence, 'A Place to Play', *The Times*, 30 August 1958.
116 Interview with Tricia (Castlemilk, b.1957), 2015.

4 Communities

Identity, change and neighbourly relations

In histories of post-war reconstruction, as well as within wider popular memory, an enduring premise of the high-rise failure argument is that multi-storey estates 'destroyed communities'. According to this perspective, while post-war planners imagined the flatted estate as a utopia of neighbourly interdependence, in reality the design and layout of modernist and high-rise estates impeded the reconstruction of 'traditional' working-class communities, producing instead atomised 'inner-city' populations scarred by crime, violence and substance abuse. During the 1970s and 1980s, when many British cities were perceived to be in the grip of a nation-wide 'urban crisis', such a view came to exemplify popular representations of Glasgow's high-rise legacy. Major developments such as Red Road and Queen Elizabeth Square in the Gorbals, initially celebrated as marking a new dawn in the city's long history of poor housing, were cited as paradigm examples of social alienation and community disintegration within the wider national debate on the failure of post-war housing policy.[1]

This chapter tells a different story about the development of community life on Glasgow's high-rise estates. Using residents' personal accounts to reconstruct a detailed history of neighbourly relations on such estates, we suggest that the narrative of community failure has overlain and obscured a more complex social history of community development. Contrary to the view of contemporary commentators and experts, we argue in the first part of this chapter that community life was in fact re-created on many estates during their early years, albeit in a way that reflected the growing post-war importance of privacy and personal autonomy in shaping residents' use and evaluation of domestic space. In this regard, neighbourly relations on high-rise estates mirrored wider trends whereby post-war economic and residential change transformed the nature of community life without destroying it, expanding the possibilities for more voluntaristic and personalised forms of social relationship without obliterating everyday connectivities and solidarities.[2] What emerges is a story of adaptation, whereby community life was reconstituted via an articulation between pre-existing aspects of 'face-to-face community' and enhanced post-war impulses towards individualism.

Over time, however, as on many other council estates, such solidarities ultimately proved vulnerable to disruption. The second part of this chapter uses personal accounts of residential change to explore how the forms of community life established during the early years of settlement were progressively undermined, engendering a pervasive narrative of communal loss and decline. This, we contend, was not an inexorable outcome of intrinsic design flaws – although as we have seen already in this book, the design of interior and exterior spaces did place strains on communality – but was contingent upon changes in the way estates were managed and the impact this had upon neighbourly relations and high-rise estates' reputational devaluation. The creeping residualisation of public housing and especially high-rise flats, whereby the tenure was repurposed as a safety-net service for individuals incapable of affording private sector housing, dramatically transformed the social composition of many estates whilst intensifying the class stigma associated with multi-storey housing almost from its inception. Instead of a story of inevitable community failure, residents' accounts reveal a complex process of social change where class, as both an economic and cultural process, exercised a powerful influence over the changing experience and evaluation of community life.

Eventless places? Neighbourly interactions on high-rise estates

Amongst other things, critics of the high-rise revolution drew attention to what they perceived as high-rise living's damaging effects upon the communal ethos and habits of the city's 'traditional' working-class neighbourhoods. According to one local journalist, reporting his impressions of the new 17-storey blocks established at Roystonhill in 1962, 'the easy neighbourliness of the ordinary Glasgow tenement' was rendered 'difficult if not impossible' by the 'sheer size of the big blocks', creating an anonymous environment akin to a 'human anthill'.[3] Similarly, an internal local authority report drafted by Glasgow Corporation's Department of Architecture and Design perceived that 'life within a multi-storey block can be a most lonely existence',[4] a view echoed by Jephcott in her own survey of the city's new high-rise estates:

> Another of the social disabilities of the high flat is that it is excessively self-contained. It has none of the neutral areas, doorstep, yard or garden, which help people to build up dossiers on each other

without necessarily exchanging a word. And it is blind in that its windows afford no two-way link with the outside world. This turns the block and estate into eventless places, shorn of those goings-on of life that tempt people out of their homes, give them shared interests and help them strike up acquaintance should they so wish.[5]

This equation, between multi-storey design and social withdrawal, quickly gained ground in public discussions of the city's high-rise revolution during the late 1960s and early 1970s. Yet, while it was certainly true that modern flats enmeshed residents within new orderings of domestic space, as the environment around the Wyndford-Daleside flats depicted in Figure 4.1 shows, it was by no means clear that social alienation was an inexorable outcome. Residential adaptation, often in unfamiliar localities, certainly incurred frustrations, losses and loneliness. As observed in Chapters 2 and 3, the challenges of living high for many new residents coupled with the location of some estates, lack of amenities and maintenance failures, could result in a retreat into the flat and a decline in communal cooperation and sociability. In general, however, the notion that the design and layout of high-rise developments encouraged immediate social disintegration

Figure 4.1 Tower blocks in Wyndford-Daleside.

conflicts with how many early high-rise dwellers narrated the problems and possibilities posed by their new residential environments. The tendency of contemporary critics to contrast the atomising effects of high-rise living with 'traditional' tenement communality constituted a misreading of residents' valuation of domestic space and experience of their former housing. Multi-storey flats did enable and encourage residents' embrace of new forms of privacy and seclusion: a common refrain amongst high-rise dwellers was 'we enjoy the privacy'. Thus, Mr Eaves, who moved to Dougrie Road, Castlemilk, with his young family in 1965, compared his new dwelling to 'a big luxury hotel', where the limitation of neighbourly contact enabled his enjoyment of a more home-centred lifestyle:

> No dislikes at all. I know by sight most of the people in the block but I don't know them well. I think this detached form of living is what people really want. I think it is so much better than being in and out of people's houses all the time ... I'm very thankful to be here. I'd like to see a cinema and a public house here. I think it's a beautiful place to live, it's always quiet, I love to come home here.[6]

However, while critics interpreted such 'detachment' as symptomatic of communal disruption, the widespread valorisation of privacy was in fact a response to the forced character of tenement communality and the various deprivations it entailed. Modern multi-storey flats merely supplied a context in which many working-class people could, for the first time, achieve a measure of control over the fashioning of their domestic environments and how they interacted with neighbours as Chapter 2 has described, marking both an enhancement in personal autonomy and their sense of social respectability.

Accordingly, the main source of communal tension on many flatted estates concerned, not so much excessive home-centredness, but perceived threats to the 'respectability' of the estate deriving from neighbours' failure to 'respect' the 'privacy' of others. A ubiquitous feature of early responses to Glasgow's new flatted estates was complaints against neighbours, children and 'hooligans' whose behaviour breached norms of communal respectability. According to Mr Boddie, who moved with his family to the Wyndford Estate in 1963:

> It is a pity, they had two nice little squares planted with roses but they had to brick it up because they were always wasted. We were promised that the area of grass we look out onto would be landscaped. Now it is used for the boys playing football. We can't open our verandah windows because of the language used by the hooligans, many of

them don't belong to the scheme. When we told them to play somewhere else we got gun-shot pellets through the windows, and we have
had another window broken by a golf ball. On Sunday afternoons it is
so noisy.[7]

Where critics such as Jephcott worried about the de-personalising effects of
excessive home-centredness, the concerns of Mr Boddie allude to a different
kind of problem: defensibility. Flats offered residents new forms of privacy,
but, given the integrated nature of multi-storey housing, the maintenance of
such privacies was necessarily dependent upon neighbourly conformity and
co-operation. In this regard, multi-story design potentially encouraged the
external enforcement of collective norms associated with community life in
tenement and other forms of pre-war working-class housing. One implication
of this, intimated in Mr Boddie's observations, was that the figure of the 'bad
neighbour' loomed large in the collective imagination of high-rise dwellers,
as a 'disrespectful' neighbour could have a disproportionate impact on the
harmony of neighbourhood life.

A different implication, however, was that privacy and reciprocity often
co-existed in a delicate balance on many, if not all, estates. Complaints
about neighbourly transgression should not be read merely as symptoms of
communal division but as evidence of a micro-politics of residential space
essential to the construction of social boundaries and common to estate
living more generally.[8] Such boundaries, enforced by estate managers,
caretakers as well as vigilant neighbours, set limits on everyday behaviour
and often produced friction between residents. Steven Cairns, whose
parents moved with his family to a high flat in Glenfinnan Road on the
Wyndford estate in 1962, became aware of the disciplinary functions of
communal surveillance when he scored a makeshift crossbar on the base
of his block:

the local copper at that time would be a guy called Frank Ryan, he
was the bobby. And coppers in those days had a kind of militaristic,
straight down the line, no left or right, you do what you do or there's
big trouble. And he caught me one day, I was only about four, or five
years old. And I was- we always used to kick a ball about, that's what
you did, you got a pal and you'd play football. And we – if you look
at the bottom of the building there's lots of concrete supports on the
bottom of the building, so the spacing between these was ideal as a
goalpost. But we would always argue, 'Where's the top of the goalpost?' So I picked up a wee stone or whatever it was and made a wee
mark on the concrete. And he must have saw me from a distance and
he came right over and he was so harsh, I just remember him saying

'You, go and tell the caretaker right now what you've done and you go and get a bucket and a mop and clean that' and I remember I thought, if I don't do that I'm gonnae go to prison. So I remember standing outside the caretaker's door – caretakers in these days lived on the block, they had the flat position 1B, all the caretakers lived in flat position 1B in all of these blocks. So I remember sittin' ootside his door, greetin' [crying] as a wee child not knowing what to do, I was just in a quandary, and eventually somebody opened the door. And it was John Lyall. John Lyall was a – he was a strict man as well. And I tried to tell him what had happened. And he's like, 'I'm no givin' you a mop and bucket, you get your mother to do it.' So not just him I had to tell, I had to tell my mother as well.[9]

Yet, while the enforcement of social and spatial norms could have punitive implications, boundary-making did not preclude neighbourly interaction and reciprocity; on the contrary, it supplied the terms within which neighbourliness was defined and shared practices formulated. Alongside the valorisation of privacy, a common perception concerned the positive relationship between spatial intimacy, familiarity and the mutuality of neighbourly relations. According to Mr Welch, whose family moved to the Moss Heights development in 1958:

I mean the Moss Heights was a village at that time, I suppose it's a bit of a cliché, but it was a vertical village. And like a traditional village, if you lived in the one close with people you would have quite close relationships with them. You'd know, quite well, families and people in adjacent closes, and even people from the other block, you would know quite well.[10]

Similarly, Lorraine, whose family moved to Castlemilk in 1966, recalled that:

you knew everybody, we were in an in-shot [corner flat] so my mum had, we'd a door and a door, as in we were in the corner, the other one out in the main, and then you had two pensioners' houses, and then you had the other main and you would have another one in an in-shot.[11]

Such intimacies, based in the first instance on spatial proximity, evolved in a variety of ways. If multi-storey housing enabled the creation of new privacies, tenants' contracts with the local authority also enshrined collective obligations to preserve the physical fabric and social standing of new estates. One expression of this was the mandatory cleaning of stairwells, landings and other communal spaces within blocks, activities typically undertaken by women. Such tasks could be frustrating, particularly when a 'bad neighbour' failed to 'take their turn', but they also generated shared routines, interdependencies and standards between neighbours, at least in the early years. Betty Williamson, who moved to the Wyndford Estate in 1963, recalled how her neighbours developed their own system for maintaining the 'respectability' of their floor, replicating a practice common in pre-war tenement housing.

> Well there was four of us. So, each of us had a turn a week. So, once every four weeks was your turn. And it was a card, and when I done it, I put it through the next one's door to remind them that was their turn for that.[12]

In a different way, contacts and affective relationships grew out of diverse forms of everyday voluntary exchange. Often, these were conditioned by shared economic needs and the gendered division of domestic labour. For Betty, neighbourly relations became especially important following the birth of her daughter, an event which removed her from the labour market at the same time as it created new financial strains. One morning she fell into conversation with Margaret, a mother living three floors down, in a communal space peculiar to the high-rise estate: the basement laundry room:

> I noticed that she had the baby and I had a lot of clothes belonging to Kirsty and I says to her, I says, 'I don't want you to be offended but I've got a lot of baby clothes'. I says, 'And I don't want to throw then out cause a lot of them are still quite brand new'. She went, 'Nae problem'. And that was, and we kept doing that so we did for years. Aye, we never, Kirsty grew out her stuff and then Susan started catching up so it was the opposite way. (Laughs)[13]

In addition to sharing clothes, Margaret and Betty developed their own system for sharing childcare routines, enabling each of them to take up part-time work without resort to 'babysitters':

> she had two wee ones and she was in the same position as me. So, we couldnae afford babysitters and what we done was I got a job from nine o'clock to half past twelve and she got a job half past one to half past four.

> Interviewer: Right. So what you did was then ...

Kept each other's kids.[14]

At other times, affective relationships and informal sharing practices were fostered by perceptions of religious communality. This was significant in Glasgow where religious allegiances were often spatially defined. When Mrs Thallon first moved to Moss Heights in 1975 she initially encountered her downstairs neighbour as something of a nuisance:

> when we moved in here he was a funny man, ah mean, a couple of times he used to come to the door and say, eh, 'You're letting water in, in mah bathroom', ah says, well funny enough mah youngest son was always in the bath when he would come up an ah wid say, 'Michael is there any water in the floor in there?' An' he says, 'is that that old pest again!'[15]

However, once Mr McKenna realised his upstairs neighbours were co-religionists his attitude softened, at least in the perception of Mrs Thallon's husband: 'it wis funny the first time he saw us going tae Lourdes Church he started tae speak tae us. An' mah husband always maintained that it was because we wur Catholics that he started tae speak tae us.' Thenceforth, Mr McKenna became a regular fixture in the Thallon family home, ascending the stairwell each night around eight o'clock to engage in some form of barter, borrowing or gift-giving. When he discovered Mrs Thallon's husband worked in Bar & Strouds, an optical engineering firm, Mr McKenna asked him a favour:

> he asked Peter if he could get him a pair o' binoculars, you know. Well, they sold them, but you hid tae do it all private with the firm. An' eh, when he got them, ah mean, they were oh, they were all lovely done, in a lovely leather case. Mr McKenna, you used to see him at night, out in the, you know, wae the binoculars, looking all over the place.[16]

In return, Mr McKenna brought gifts for Mrs Thallon's boys:

> He came up then wae a bag a used golf balls for the boys. An' eh, gave, ah think it wis one o' the boys, he gave him wellingtons or something for going, whatever they use to go, hiking and different things.[17]

Perhaps most obviously, however, the most cohesive and multifaceted forms of social network emerged where individuals were connected through a lattice of intersecting relationships. Lorraine recalled her block in Castlemilk as the fulcrum of a set of different relationships central to her memories of growing up. One world was that of school and its overlap with 'the flats' as a locus of play:

> it was the same people that, that you played with, you widnae play with them all, but, well it was the same thing, it was me an' Susan, there was another couple o' lassies but we were a wee crowd, that we all stayed in the flats ..., an' then the thing was, they were my, some of they were my friends but they, they lived in different bits but my da worked in British Telecom with them so my dad knew their dads.[18]

As Lorraine goes on to explain, however, her relationship with school-friends was also reinforced by the fact that so many men in the building worked for British Telecom. This meant that 'my dad knew their dads', as drinking partners as well as co-workers and neighbours:

> Yip, they were all in Telecom which was down at the bottom of the hill, that was the main ...
>
> Interviewer: So they all went out to the pub?
>
> Yip, they all went tae the Labour Club which they walked down tae, the Labour Club was, that was just along, straight along ...[19]

Finally, Lorraine recalled the domestic world of her mother and the friend-ships she formed with other women in the block:

> my mum was friends with the person in six, in number six, they would go up, up an' down, who was next door to my friend. So them three were like, there was my friend Susan an' then there was a lady called Mrs Wilson. So we were two above her but my mum an' her used to go tae one another's houses on a Friday night ... an' as I say my friend's mum, ah mean they were friendly with her as well. I remember they went in tae the Tenants' Association and things like that.[20]

Multi-storey flats were not then 'eventless places, shorn of those goings-on of life that tempt people out of their homes, give them shared interests and help them strike up acquaintance'.[21] On the contrary, flatted estates, like post-war estates more generally, were places rich in social life, where resi-dents fashioned meaningful relationships, belongings and attachments. The crucial difference was that, by comparison with the enforced communality characteristic of Glasgow's tenements, these relationships were increasingly personalised and voluntaristic, even as the spatial intimacies of high-rise living entailed the enduring importance of neighbourly co-operation as a facet of everyday life. That contemporary social observers routinely misread this adaptation for social disintegration says more about the normative models of 'community' they projected onto working-class housing, than the social effects of modernist housing itself. Once this dissonance between public critique and lived experience is recognised, the inevitability of 'community break-down' becomes questionable, opening space for a properly historical explanation that illuminates the contingencies of social change.

Narratives of community loss and decline

The Ronan Point disaster of 1968, in which a gas explosion killed four high-rise dwellers in Newham, London represents a symbolic turning point within conventional historical narratives of the 'British high-rise experiment'.[22] For critics, then and now, the event exposed the inherent dangers of high-rise living and signalled the beginning of the end of the British municipal embrace of multi-storey housing. As such, Ronan Point has formed a powerful signifying element within a tightly compressed history of the decline of high-rise housing in which intrinsic design and technical failures caused immediate and inevitable degeneration. This narrative of inevitable failure continues to have a powerful purchase on the popular imagination, encouraging its periodic deployment by elite politicians. Writing in the *Sunday Times* as recently as January 2016, British Prime Minister David Cameron argued for the obliteration of Britain's 'sink estates' in well-worn terms:

> within these so-called sink estates, behind front doors, families build warm and welcoming homes. But step outside in the worst estates, and you're confronted by concrete slabs dropped from on high, brutal high-rise towers and dark alleyways that are a gift to criminals and drug dealers. The police often talk about the importance of designing out crime, but these estates actually designed it in.[23]

Analysis of residents' experiences in the Glasgow context suggests a more complex and longer-term picture of the degeneration of the city's high-rise developments. Consideration of the historical trajectory of even a small proportion of the city's high-rise estates complicates any notion of a uniform history of residential decline: different developments evolved in different ways, at different rates, yielding different long-run outcomes. In some instances, major developments appear to have experienced debilitating social problems virtually from the point of opening. In 1967 Brian Trevor moved with his family from a single-end tenement in Oatlands, Rutherglen, to the nearby Toryglen estate in south Glasgow which contained three high-rise blocks surrounded by deck-access low rise housing. While the new three-bedroom flat was much more 'spacious' than the family's previous residence, it quickly became apparent 'the way the place was going':

> By about 1974 we found it was becoming a really toxic place to stay, you know the lifts were being used as toilets by people. Dogs were supposed to have been banned but they seemed to start a process of housing what I suppose you'd call 'anti-social tenants', who had dogs in the flats and the council never really did anything about that. You found, even on the stairs, human waste on the stairs, needles, used needles on the stairs. They tried to put in a controlled entry system around '74, and again somebody smashed it in the second day, and it was never repaired, eh, it became the norm for at least one lift not to be working, and the state of the operation on the other lift, if you ever did use it, you would be mentally relieved to get out of it. So essentially, even after a few years, it was a pretty horrible place to stay. There were still some of the original tenants who tried to keep some sort of pride in their house and live a kind of life that didn't become a nuisance to others, but they were becoming fewer and fewer. There were people two floors up, young people, maybe about nineteen, they were housed in there, and then started having really noisy parties, with the windows open and stuff. And it just really became a horrible, horrible place to stay. Not a place really where I'd be keen to have friends back to, because to be honest it really became a place I was ashamed to bring anybody to.[24]

More commonly, residents' personal narratives intimate a more gradual and uneven process of social change, albeit with common themes and turning points. Long-term residents on many estates told of the erosion of neighbourly values and a loss of spatial control due to the dilution of the 'original' community by new arrivals bereft of 'respect' for their surroundings. Whereas Brian portrayed these processes as effective from the birth of the Toryglen development, the wider narrative of social degeneration shifts the precipitating events forward in time, to the 1980s and 90s. Ray Goldie recalled of Moss Heights, for example, that:

from the eighties, from about the mid, from about the mid-eighties onwards ye started to get occurrences of what ye'd call anti-social behaviour ... because every, every tenant was a kind of, you know, responsible, more or, more or less responsible conscientious kind of person. Eh, but what happened in the eighties, you started to get ... as, as the more prosperous people moved away, ye then started to get people coming in who maybe were unemployed or, or it was like, you know, single mothers or something like this you know, that, that aspect of it come into it an' you got the problems assoc-, you know often associated with this. So eh, ah mean, so ye started tae get instances of, of that an' as ah say, that's what happened here, somebody moved in upstairs.[25]

Similarly, Thomas Black depicted the 1980s as a turning point in the trajectory of the Wyndford Estate:

it must have been the nineties maybe, late eighties, early nineties, it started going downhill ... people using drugs, things like that, moving into the flats, as I say, ... people got moved in where they wanted, that sort of thing. I mean and then, it just brought the tone down for everybody else, which wasnae very fair. There was people scared to go up in the lifts and things like that. I mean the flat I stayed in, there was three murders within the space of, about six months.[26]

This collective narrative of decline needs to be approached with critical sensitivity. For, whatever its descriptive functions, it is also a form of communal memory, the distillation of which is powerfully shaped by residents' need to explain, to themselves and others, the negative changes that have transformed their estates. Necessarily, therefore, residents' stories are emotionally and culturally mediated: the version of change which residents relate is shaped in dialogue with wider cultural expectations, particularly around the relationship between housing and social class, and works to preserve a sense of personal and collective dignity separate from generalising assumptions about the 'types' of people who live in high-rise housing. Hence, echoing the moral distinctions evoked in David Cameron's story of innocent families besieged by criminals and deviants, this narrative relates the fall of an intrinsically respectable community that, through no fault of its own, has been abandoned by the state, contaminated by 'foreign' incursions, and misjudged by outsiders. In situating their personal experiences within this alternative collective narrative, long-term residents thus differentiate themselves from publicly stigmatised lifestyles associated with 'inner-city' decay, and instead identify themselves with the 'decency' of the first generation of residents.

What is important here is that this way of narrating the history of one's estate constitutes a re-negotiation of residents' social identities in response to a pattern of social change common to many estates, not just high rise. Central to this was the relationship between the perceived social identity of new neighbours and municipal allocation practices. As Brian put it, 'there was a very definite policy of, which had been operating for a long time, housing, you know, the anti-social tenants in the one area, and that's principally what made it such a horrific place to stay'.[27]

As sociologist Sean Damer has shown, 'filtering' tenants by social class was integral to municipal housing governance in Glasgow in the 1930s, and the practice was re-established after 1945 despite the universalist premises undergirding the post-war expansion of public housing.[28] In relation to the city's high-rise revolution, however, the social identities of multi-storey tenants as whole were subject to stigmatisation virtually from the inception of the process. One reason for this was that high-rise estates, despite being promoted as a new departure, were popularly identified with the 'slum' populations many were created to re-house amidst an intensive programme of 'comprehensive redevelopment' within the city's inner-zone. Buttressed by a selective 'overspill' policy, implemented as part of a regional strategy of modernisation geared to the relocation of Glasgow's industry and population to new towns, this induced a massive out-migration of skilled workers and young families, resulting in a concentration of manual workers and old people within the city's new peripheral and inner-city estates. Thus this process narrowed the economic background of multi-storey residents and fostered the transposition of the stigma of the 'slum' onto new high-rise estates.[29] Hence, only years after opening, many high-rise blocks were branded 'vertical slums of the future' in the local press, and attempts by the council to site new developments in 'respectable' middle-class areas were instinctively resisted by private residents' associations who feared flat-dwellers were likely to be a 'different sort of people', possessing 'a different way of life' having come 'from Glasgow's tenements, into houses which were the modern concept of the tenement'.[30]

More generally, these processes anticipated wider shifts in housing policy which recast public housing as a vehicle for addressing a range of social problems associated with homelessness, vagrancy, ill-health and single-parent families.[31] While the effects of this shift were uneven, affecting different estates at different times, legislative and funding changes to public housing from the late 1960s registered a growing political commitment to the residualisation of public housing: the strategic repurposing of the tenure as a safety-net service for individuals incapable of house purchase. This was reflected, not only in incentives to private home-ownership, but in the transfer of responsibility for housing the homeless to local housing authorities, successive rent hikes which squeezed 'affluent' tenants from the tenure, and the expansion of 'priority needs' criteria for filtering assess to the tenure.[32]

The implications of these combined processes for the subsequent social and cultural history of Glasgow's multi-storey estates were multi-faceted and far-reaching. While residualisation theoretically affected all social housing tenants, 'vulnerable' tenants were often concentrated in multi-storey developments, due partially to their stigmatisation and to the associated difficulties of letting dwellings on some estates. This was comparatively cost effective and helped preserve the reputation of 'good' estates, but pre-existing tenants often perceived the arrival of new 'types' as signalling a deterioration in social status, engendering aspirations to move. When Leslie Welch's family moved to the Moss Heights development it had initially satisfied their aspirations for better quality housing (they had left behind their owner-occupied tenement in a less desirable part of the city), and their neighbours were regarded as 'good sorts'. However, by the late 1960s the Welch's had identified a marked shift in the estate's social standing:

the whole place was as good as the weakest member of the village, as it were. And I do think, you know, as time went by, that there was more incidence of you know, drink problems, of vandalism, of – not violence, but you know, disputes within families and that kind of thing. So all the sort of, quality of the social environment was deteriorating.[33]

Moreover, at the same time as Moss Heights was losing its appeal, home ownership was being promoted as an attractive and realisable housing option for a much broader cross-section of British society.[34] Increasingly, high-rise estates formed the popular antithesis of the aspirational ideals embodied in the figure of the 'home owner' – even in Glasgow which traditionally had the highest proportion of renters in the UK – while 'owner occupation' was fast becoming a necessary condition of respectable status for upwardly mobile households, as recognised by Leslie Welch:

But you know there was, at that point also this sort of increase in the desire to own your own property, it first started around then. Because historically, Glasgow's not like that, it was, you know, more a central European model of tenements and stuff like that. And I think, particularly they [parents] thought having sent us to the grammar school, we

were mixing with people who – we were the only people who were
coming from …

Interviewer: A high-rise building.

Yeah, everyone else was coming from Newton Mearns and Giffnock
[middle-class suburbs] and that sort of thing. I think in the same way
they sent us to grammar school, I think they sort of felt they needed to
basically buy a house and join that sort of …[35]

For other tenants, however, many of whose working lives were impacted
by Glasgow's accelerating de-industrialisation, entry into the private
market was much less realisable. For these long-term residents, the shifts
in estate composition shaped by residualisation altered the conduct of
neighbourhood life in diverse ways. Often, new arrivals were perceived to
undermine pre-existing codes, networks and attachments, and sometimes
rendered particular floors and blocks as threatening spaces. While Betty
Williamson, who had lived in her flat for 37 years, retained highly positive
memories of her time in the Wyndford, as a long-term resident she was
able to recount the changes in neighbourhood life. Like many others we
spoke to, Betty identified the decline in communal cleaning routines as
symptomatic of broader changes affecting the estate since the 1980s.

I mean, when I was working full time, eh, (pause) there was a wee
woman, again it kept a lot of pensioners. They went out and done the
stairs, a couple of pound, gave them that wee bit extra in their pocket.
Then, it was two pound a month you would give her. And, when the
contract took over it was five pound a month. Now it's nearly eight
pound a month. And that's not even with them saying, 'Do you want
to do this?' You're getting told because there's that many bad tenants.
That way – 'You'll all pay'…. Eh, as I say, they kept, they really did,
the upkeep was really great, but now it's odds and sods that are
going in.
    As I say, it's the people who, it's don't get me wrong it's not all
the people that's in them. But there's that element who you just don't
want to know. You just don't want to know them.[36]

Despite the popular tendency to associate modernist housing with homogeni-
sation, the dwelling specifications of blocks on many Glasgow estates were
differentiated by designers' perceptions of the different needs and life-style
preferences of discrete tenant groups. One reflection of this was the inclusion
of clusters of single-person dwellings within blocks, often interposed with

larger family dwellings, to cater for pensioners who, as they got older, were increasingly vulnerable to problems of loneliness and isolation. Following the commencement of residualisation, however, an unforeseen consequence of this design choice was that these single-person dwellings were often seen by housing managers as ideal accommodation for high 'priority needs' young people. These new tenants, who often inhabited dwellings for a relatively short period of time before moving elsewhere, were much less invested in maintaining long-established routines, such as cleaning stairwells, and in Lorraine's view they unravelled the close-knit familiarity of inter-personal relations on her family's floor. More disconcertingly, many of the new arrivals, few of whom were in employment, threw loud parties through the week, and eventually Lorraine's mother arrived home one afternoon to find her well-bolted flat burgled:

> they bust it, they halfed the door, that was quite, we, we'd quite a lot of locks. Most people just had a Yale, all my pals had one key, we'd three. My ma had a lock up the top, a Yale and then a lock, a double lock down the bottom. And they actually, it was like as though they'd put a jemmy and snapped the door in two and they were big solid doors.[37]

A similar pattern of events was related by Steven Cairns, who, like Lorraine, expressed a strong sense of belonging to the neighbourhood in which he grew up on the Wyndford Estate. During the 1980s, however, the management of the estate was transferred to a new private housing association, at which point Steven began to notice a change in the 'people that are coming in'. For Steven, this led to a 'nightmare scenario' when a long-term and trusted neighbour moved flats:

> my neighbour, next door, she would have moved in at the same time as my parents. And when she got older, this would be mid-nineties, she realised that she had to move to another flat which was on a landing, cos she couldn't do the stairs, the connecting stairs. So they moved her, and the first family to replace her was a woman with two of the most (sighs) *wild* kids. One would be about ten and the other about fifteen, and the one at fifteen had a drug problem. He was a *junkie*. And the mother was- you could see she was uneducated, you could see she was not a nice person. Not a nice person at all. And I could see straightaway that she wasn't in control of her children. So they started, I suppose, messin' the place up. Vandalising the place- eh, I came home from work one day ... and the fifteen-year-old son of this woman was sittin' on the landing stairs with one of his mates with

a bottle of whiskey and they'd just pissed all over the landing. As I said, we'd never had this before ... I said 'listen, I'm no accepting this mate, this is not gonna happen here, I'm not allowin' you to do this, you know, and I'm gonna deal with it' and eh I just got a lot of verbal abuse, straight away and physical threat. You know, for example they said 'well who the fuck are you, we know where you live, we'll do you in mate' and I'm like 'oh really, okay'. So I left it at that, I stopped the conversations, I knew exactly where this was goin.[38]

Following this altercation, Steven was torn by conflicting emotions. For although he resented his new neighbours' lack of respect for a place he regarded as home, he lived in fear of retributive violence should he become embroiled in further confrontation. Consequently, Steven was forced to become a virtual 'private investigator', monitoring and gathering evidence on his neighbour's behaviour in order to persuade the management company to reallocate the family. This, however, took two years:

So I thought, how do I deal with this? So I was from that point on physically threatened and I'm thinkin' this could all go pretty horrible, how do you deal with this? So I had to work out how I could get my housing association to help me. And they didn't really help me that much. And housing policy was *against* me. So it took a lot, it took a lot. You know, of documenting everything that was goin' on, creating a diary. All these things you shouldn't have to do. And it took a couple of years for them to get moved on.[39]

In turn, the long-run effect of these processes has been to fundamentally transform Steven's perception of an environment he has lived in all his life. Where Glenfinnan Road appears as a place of community and sanctuary in Steven's account of his earlier life, the need to manage the threat posed by the influx of tenants with 'big problems' has created a dehumanised environment, where technological boundary formation has replaced voluntaristic social boundaries, and where once-familiar spaces now evoke insecurity, anxiety and anonymity:

when they started changin' the rules then it was like these barriers got put up, you got the entry system, you got the security, you got the cameras, you got these strange people comin' in you don't know, and there's no names on the doors, no names on any doors now, so you don't know who you're neighbours are. And to me, that is what's eroding, it's an erosion. And it's not good, it's not healthy, its turnin' the block into a kind of faceless, almost prison-like environment.[40]

The narratives of Steven, Lorraine and Betty, Brian and Thomas, Leslie and Ray, thus register an alternative history of 'community failure' on Glasgow's multi-storey estates. When residents first moved into their new flats in the 1960s residential change was then defined in terms of improvement: at this historical moment, the benefits of high-rise estates were interpreted in relation to prior housing experiences, within the context of residents' memories of living in Glasgow's industrial tenements. Given subsequent changes in the governance, composition and reputation of many estates, however, this initial structure of feeling was gradually displaced by a new one. Perspectives constructed from the vantage point of the present contrast the respectability and sociability of flatted estates during early settlement with the absence of these virtues in the present, the memory of tenement life having progressively faded as a framework of comparative evaluation. The crucial point is that, while the buildings have in many instances remained the same, residualisation transformed the lived experience of neighbourhood life whilst intensifying negative societal perceptions of the social identity of high-rise populations. The figure of the 'problem tenant' mobilised in these accounts thus refracts a more fundamental story of abandonment, loss and shame concerning the fragmentation of local networks, managerial indifference, and the erosion of 'respectable' class status.

New neighbourly relations

It is important to note, however, that the effects of residualisation, pervasive though they were, did not take the same form for every long-term high-rise dweller. While all residents agreed that their estates had 'gone downhill' as a whole, at the micro-level of floors and blocks some tenants emphasised the enduring stability of neighbourly relations due to neighbours having bought their flats and remained on the estate. Betty Williamson described herself as 'very fortunate' in having long-standing neighbours on her floor and when one long term friend died she found the new tenant was easy to get to know.[41] In a different way, other residents found themselves warming to their new neighbours, forming new relationships despite initial misgivings. Mrs Mary Thallon had lived in her flat at Moss Heights for some 40 years when she was interviewed in 2015. During that time, Mrs Thallon's husband had died, her two sons had moved away, and few of her original neighbours remained on her block: 'ah mean, to me they were used to being there, you knew every neighbour up the entrance but now, I mean, as I say there's only about five or six you know, the same as us, so'.[42]

Despite this dissipation of familiar faces, however, Mrs Thallon spoke warmly of many of her new neighbours, depicting them as sources of kindness, conversation and support. Jane and Matthew, for example, introduced themselves in the lift:

> Even the other day I came in the lift and a young couple came in at six, and eh, she said, eh, she says, 'We've just moved in at Christmas.' I had never seen the girl before. She said 'I think I met you once in the lift' she says, 'but we've just moved in.' I said 'Oh I don't remember seeing ye', but she just said to me 'I'm Jane and this is Matthew, my husband', and we just shook hands. And she says, 'well we can speak now that we've met, you know.' Well, I said 'That's better than standing in the lift and just looking at each other', you know. But as I say everybody seems to be quite friendly you know.[43]

Similarly, the new family next door regularly helped with running errands and household chores, in the absence of Mrs Thallon's own sons:

> they are really good, I mean, if when the weather's bad I only need to knock the door and the boys'll go and get me something you know, like during the day because my sons are all working you know. But even that, if Jamie's home and the weather's bad he'll phone and say ye better not go out it's too slippy. 'Do ye need milk or anything? Later on I'll, I'll come up and get it'. But the boys next door, I mean they're, they're really good, I mean, if a bulb goes out I only need to knock the door and they come in and put a bulb in, you know. I say, well it's silly to go and phone my son away down here to come and put a bulb in you know, two seconds, you know but. Ah mean, the mother and father always say that, anything you need, or anytime you need any help just knock the door, you know, so.[44]

And on a frosty Sunday morning a previously 'surly' new neighbour ferried Mrs Thallon to church, changing her perceptions and kindling new affections:

> And that was like one Sunday I was goin' to mass it was, it was quite slippy and I had went along the avenue but at the bend of the avenue at the very end, I looked and I said oh I said I don't think I'll be able to cross there. So, there was a taxi sitting, I had seen the taxi there nearly every morning and I just went to the taxi man and I says 'I wonder if you could give me a lift tae the church, tae Lourdes Avenue?' And he says 'oh yes', so it wasn't 'till I went into the car and I looked and it was the man, one of the Pakistanis down in, think it's three is it he stays. And he took me right tae Lourdes Avenue and

I said to him … he says 'oh no no' and it was then that ah realised who he was, he says 'It's quite all right, you're my neighbour so I've done you a favour.' And I went 'Ooohhhh' [intake of breath?] I said 'oh I'm …', I said 'I thought you were a taxi!', he said 'no'.

Interviewer: You hadn't recognised him [laughing]

[laughs] Well, you know how in the morning it was quite dark then you know, and he, when I offered to pay him for taking me tae the church he said no, you are my neighbour and I went, 'oh it's you', and yet that man used tae come in the lift and was quite surly in the morning. If he would say good morning he would say 'morning' [in low gruff voice] and see now, oh he talks away tae ye…. I said, och well, maybe it was meant tae happen. Ye need tae be friendly towards people, you know, so, that was us.[45]

Personal narratives of place can be analysed to reveal broad shifts in popular consciousness, but they can also be analysed at the level of individual housing journeys. At the former scale, the focus is on the shared images and tropes which organise perceptions collectively and how these mutate over time. At the latter scale, the focus is on how the specificity of lived experience produces variation in collective histories. Mrs Thallon's account of change at Moss Heights, read at this latter scale, demonstrates the limits of any universalising history of residualisation. In her narrative loss did not centre on issues of respectability or social class, but instead sprang from the emotional ramifications of life-cycle transition and the dispersal of close family members. In negotiating these ramifications, intimated in the signs of loneliness which permeate her anecdotes, Mrs Thallon recognises 'ye need tae be friendly towards people', and, given caring and receptive neighbours, has been able to fashion supportive relationships with a new and different generation of tenants. For Mrs Thallon, therefore, her new neighbours are a source of comfort rather than instability, and her personal experiences illuminate fragments of a more variegated pattern of neighbourly relations, where forms of intergenerational renewal co-exist with the more destructive effects of long-term residualisation and stigmatisation.

Conclusions: retelling the history of community life

In an influential essay, the historical geographer Doreen Massey has interrogated the intimate connection between place and storytelling. Histories of place, she reminds us, are never mere chronologies of physical spaces;

they participate, rather, in the very constitution of places: 'The identity of places is very much bound up with the *histories* which are told of them, *how* those histories are told, and which may turn out to be dominant.'[46] Within contemporary British society, the identity of the multi-storey flat has long been defined by a history narrated by experts, politicians and journalists. In this account, brutalist design fantasies spawned a generation of 'failed communities', the legacies of which continue to malign Britain's inner cities up to the present day. The histories told by high-rise dwellers, however, relate a more complex story.

Where early critics condemned the atomising effects of multi-storey housing, viewing estates as 'eventless places', residents' accounts portray a story of communal adaptation, where neighbours formed meaningful relationships and developed a strong sense of belonging to their estates. Whilst expert analyses identified social degeneration with intrinsic design flaws, entailing the notion of inevitable community break-down, residents' narratives repeatedly evidence a two-decade lag between the early years of residential settlement and the later deterioration of social life. In explaining this, residents emphasise neither design problems nor physical deterioration, but a historically contingent process: the effects of a policy of residualisation whereby the social composition of estates underwent dramatic transformation, undermining the stability of established neighbourly relations.

These submerged histories in turn demonstrate the importance of another element, namely the workings of social identity, as a factor structuring the social history of flatted communities. In particular, residents' narratives evidence how the experience, workings and popular understanding of community life on high-rise estates were affected by the meanings of social class. From the start, this was manifest in the expert models of 'community' against which flatted populations were found lacking, yet which were, at the same time, blind to residents' capacity to adapt to their new environments and form meaningful interpersonal relationships. It was also manifest in how flatted populations were established, dwellings allocated, and estates managed. Most importantly, it was manifest in how multi-storey estates were denigrated within wider society and culture, and in how residents, interacting with these wider discourses, located themselves and 'other' tenants within powerful typologies of social class to explain change as 'decline' and to manage the effects of stigmatisation on their psychological wellbeing.

Residents' experience of 'community' thus always involved more than enmeshment in an abstract network of inter-personal relations; it depended also on the languages of social identity through which they interpreted the personal and collective significance of those relations and evaluated the place of their community in the wider world. In this regard, the effects of residualisation need to be read, not only in terms of the destabilising effects of changing allocation practices upon neighbourhood life, but as part of a much wider process by which housing form and tenure are implicated in the imagining, assignment and everyday practice of class identities in post-war Britain. Where owner occupation has become 'normal' in contemporary society, public housing, and in particular multi-storey council housing, has been systematically devalued, such that renting within the tenure now forms a chief indicator of class difference. High rise did not achieve a status as a 'modern' form of living that could have equalised housing conditions across social classes. Instead, in Glasgow, the multi-storeys became synonymous with deprivation. What this chapter contends, however, is that this was neither inevitable nor reducible to the omnipotent effects of one isolated factor such as design.

Notes

1   For a summary of the rise and fall of Red Road see https://municipaldreams. wordpress.com/2015/10/27/the-rise-and-fall-of-the-red-road-flats-part-2-failed-postwar-visions/ (accessed 11.01.2020).
2   See, for example, Lawrence, *Me, Me, Me?* Introduction.
3   'Where High Living Falls a bit Flat', *Glasgow Herald*, 27 Dec 1962.
4   GCA, D-TC8/11/15: 'Report on Multi-storey Flats for consideration by the Housing Sub-committee on Sites and Buildings', Department of Architecture and Civic Design, July 1970.
5   Jephcott, *Homes in High Flats*, pp. 130–1.
6   UGA, DC127/1/1-10/1: Castlemilk.
7   UGA, DC127/1/1-10/1: Wyndford.
8   See, for example, Rogaly and Taylor, *Moving Histories*, pp. 68–9.
9   Interview with Steven Cairns (Wyndford, b.1962), 2015 (pseudonym).
10 Interview with Mr Leslie Welch (Moss Heights, b.1950), 2015.
11 Interview with Lorraine (Castlemilk, b.1964), 2015.
12 Interview with Mrs Betty Williamson (Wyndford, b.1949), 2015.
13 Interview with Mrs Betty Williamson (Wyndford, b.1949), 2015.
14 Interview with Mrs Betty Williamson (Wyndford, b.1949), 2015.
15 Interview with Mrs Mary Thallon (Moss Heights, b.1924), 2015.
16 Interview with Mrs Mary Thallon (Moss Heights, b.1924), 2015.
17 Interview with Mrs Mary Thallon (Moss Heights, b.1924), 2015.
18 Interview with Lorraine ((Castlemilk, b.1964), 2015.
19 Interview with Lorraine (Castlemilk, b.1964), 2015.
20 Interview with Lorraine (Castlemilk, b.1964), 2015.
21 Jephcott, *Homes in High Flats*, pp. 130–1.
22 On the symbolic importance of Ronan Point see Anne Power, *Hovels to High Rise: State Housing in Europe Since 1850* (Routledge, London, 1993); Peter Hall, *Cities of Tomorrow: An Intellectual History of Urban Planning and Design* (Wiley-Blackwell, Oxford, 1988); Ravetz, *Council Housing and Culture*.
23 David Cameron, 'Estate Regeneration', *Sunday Times*, 10 January 2016.

24 Interview with Mr Brian Trevor (Toryglen, b.1957), 2016.

25 Interview with Mr Ray Goldie (Moss Heights, b.1951), 2015.

26 Interview with Mr Thomas Black (Wyndford, b.1959), 2015.

27 Interview with Mr Brian Trevor (Toryglen, b.1957), 2016.

28 Sean Damer, '"Engineers of the human machine": The social practice of council housing management in Glasgow, 1895–1939', *Urban Studies* 37:11 (2000), pp. 2007–26. For the period after 1945 see Barry Hazley, 'Rents, Rates and Roughs: the public construction of council housing as a residual tenure in Glasgow 1945–69'. Unpublished conference paper.

29 On the socio-spatial effects of Glasgow's selective overspill policy see Collins and Levitt, 'The "modernisation" of Scotland'. See also Michael Keating, *The City that Refused to Die: Glasgow: The Politics of Urban Regeneration* (Aberdeen University Press, Aberdeen, 1988).

30 *Evening Times*, 30 April 1963 cited in Horsey, *Tenements and Towers,* p. 58. For stigmatisation within the local press more generally see, for example: 'Getting Tough with Housing Hooligans', *Glasgow Herald*, 15 March 1965; 'Problems of Housing Scheme Life', *Glasgow Herald*, 14 January 1964; 'Council Tenants get Washday Willies', *Evening Times*, 14 February 1966; 'Segregated Tenants in Glasgow? Vandals may force it', *Glasgow Herald*, 20 March 1966; 'Delinquency Problem in Glasgow', *Glasgow Herald*, 12 August 1966; 'Council Houses have to be re-let immediately to beat vandalism', *Evening Times*, 15 September 1968.

31 On the origins of the transfer of welfare responsibilities to local housing authorities see N.Crowson, 'Revisiting the 1977 Housing (Homeless Persons) Act: Westminster, Whitehall, and the homelessness lobby', *Twentieth Century British History*, 24:3 (2013), pp. 424–47.

32 On the wider development of 'residualisation' see Ben Jones, 'Slum clearance, privatization and residualization: the practices and politics of council housing in mid-twentieth-century England', *Twentieth Century British History* 21:4 (2010), pp. 510–39. For an earlier account, see Peter Malpass, *Reshaping Housing Policy: Subsidies, Rents and Residualization* (Routledge, London, 1982).

33 Interview with Mr Leslie Welch (Moss Heights, b.1950), 2015.

34 On the state-led promotion of 'owner-occupation' see Peter Saunders, *A Nation of Homeowners* (Routledge, London, 1990).

35 Interview with Mr Leslie Welch (Moss Heights, b.1950), 2015.

36 Interview with Mrs Betty Williamson (Wyndford, b.1949), 2015.

37 Interview with Lorraine (Castlemilk, b.1964), 2015.

38 Interview with Mr Steven Cairns (Wyndford, b.1962), 2015 (pseudonym).

39 Interview with Mr Steven Cairns (Wyndford, b.1962), 2015 (pseudonym).

40 Interview with Mr Steven Cairns (Wyndford, b.1962), 2015 (pseudonym).

41 Interview with Mrs Betty Williamson (Wyndford, b.1949), 2015.

42 Interview with Mrs Mary Thallon (Moss Heights, b.1924), 2015.

43 Interview with Mrs Mary Thallon (Moss Heights, b.1924), 2015.

44 Interview with Mrs Mary Thallon (Moss Heights, b.1924), 2015.

45 Interview with Mrs Mary Thallon (Moss Heights, b.1924), 2015.

46 Doreen Massey, 'Places and their pasts', *History Workshop Journal*, 39 (Spring, 1995), pp. 182–92.

Conclusions

Plural histories of multi-storey living

Glasgow's experience with high-rise housing is emblematic of the post-war embrace of multi-storey living by many British cities while also exhibiting some characteristics unique to this city. The decision to build high was made in the context of an urgent demand for new homes with modern amenities. This impetus was especially keenly felt in Glasgow where overcrowding and substandard accommodation dominated the post-war housing stock, and where poverty and deprivation were ever present. And as was the case elsewhere, blocks were erected quickly, often using untested prefabricated construction methods, and many were built in unsuitable locations. Insufficient investment in maintenance and security, absence of social amenities on many estates and, by the 1980s, new letting policies which fundamentally altered the constituency of high-rise tenants (residualisation) all contributed to a gradual decline of the environment of estates leading, on some, to a downward spiral culminating in demolition of those blocks it was deemed impossible to rescue.

Understandably, given the poor reputation of high-rise estates in the city from the 1980s onwards, when they became a byword in public discourse for deprivation, gang violence and drugs, the dominant account of multi-storey living has been one of failure. Yet, once people are added to the mix, what on the surface appears to be a wholly negative story becomes much more complex. In the wake of regeneration programmes which seek to create more liveable communities, involving the demolition of around 5,000 units or around 17 per cent of the city's high-rise flats by the end of the first decade of the twenty-first century, and the tragedy of Grenfell Tower, there is an imperative to re-evaluate the high-rise narrative in Glasgow.[1] In the preceding chapters, which listen closely to the accounts of former and present residents, we have told a more complicated story that forces a reappraisal of some of the standard interpretations of high-rise living in the post-war decades and which offers some insights regarding the factors that result in satisfaction with this particular housing model. Our findings offer a long-term temporal analysis from the first years of high rise to the present day and thus consider the specific historical context of people's reporting of their experience, contrasting the early years of the 1960s and early 1970s with retrospective accounts provided in 2015. We indicate some convergence with more recent studies undertaken in the context of regeneration of the city's social housing stock but also identify some important factors which are too frequently overlooked by those who focus on architecture and design or on the very recent past.

Even in Glasgow, where flat-dwelling in tenements of up to four storeys had been customary since the early nineteenth century, the preference was still to have one's own front door to one's own house.[2] The oft-heard complacency that Glaswegians were used to living in flats and so would easily accommodate themselves to blocks of up to 22 floors revealed a condescension for working-class tenants of social housing who, it was believed, would be so relieved at being moved from slum housing to modern flats that they would overlook the compromise this entailed. Pearl Jephcott's surprise at the overwhelming reporting of residents' 'satisfaction' with their new homes can be partly ascribed to people's lack of agency in the rehousing process and her lack of a deep understanding of the roots of this sentiment which lay in decades of failure of the local authority to address the appalling housing conditions in the city.[3] More than half a century later, programmes conducted by Glasgow Housing Association to renovate its stock, including internal and external physical renewal of high flats, had the effect of improving psychosocial outcomes for all tenants but notably, people living in high flats were significantly less likely to reap the benefits owing to the adverse effects of perceived lack of security, anti-social behaviour and 'low levels of community contact'.[4] Researchers concluded that 'In the context of Glasgow at least – a city with extensive deprivation, poor health and a poor climate – lower income groups would be better off not living in high-rise blocks.'[5]

Given the high flats are here to stay, now housing a wider range of residents from social tenants to wealthy owner-occupiers, the value of an historical approach some 60 years after the erection of the first high flats in the city is to contribute new perspectives to the evaluation of Glasgow's high-rise story. First, historians are interested in change, and continuity, over time. The history of Glasgow's high rise is not a continuous narrative of failure but contains high and low points contingent upon a range of variables from location and design to the constituency of tenants in any one block or estate. Second, historians are attentive to social, economic, political and cultural context and how this context changes over the time period and affects people's experiences and understandings of their own lives. And third, as social historians we have been concerned to give greater weight than has hitherto been the case to residents' experiences articulated in the first flush of the high-rise experiment in the city and much later with the benefit of hindsight and time to reconsider and reflect. So, we have been able to move across the temporal landscape with high-rise residents, sharing their joys and disappointments in the 1960s and then listening closely to their interpretations of why change occurred from the perspective of their current standpoint. Our analysis then draws on concepts utilised by housing scholars in the present as a lens through which to understand the past.

This perspective has produced a number of conclusions. First, the retreat to domestic privacy that the flats enabled amongst the earliest residents was appreciated and celebrated. But that privacy was compromised when the high-rise flat became a prison or a refuge from the outside. When Jephcott was interviewing residents in the 1960s the idea of the flat as a retreat was a positive and desirable aspect of the new style of living. Yet in our interviews, although people were able to recall this experience of high flat living, they also spoke with some sadness about how they or their parents had become imprisoned in the home by fear, mistrust and anxiety. Importantly, in the period of post-war affluence (both absolute and relative to wartime), as Jon Lawrence argues, culture sought to 'reconcile the twin ideals of ... [being] independent and yet also to maintain strong social connections to others – to uphold traditions of domestic privacy without becoming an island cut off from the wider world'.[6] The promise of modernist high rise was to provide the privacy and individualism that many people desired, without much concern for the other essential component, social interactions in the local neighbourhood, perhaps on the assumption that higher residential densities would necessarily result in the production or reproduction of a sense of community on estates.

In the end, high rise could not deliver on its promise in any sustained way, representing a functional form which ensured that 'it is not easy to achieve ... a happy balance between self and society'.[7] High rise is a story of promised, acquired (by some) and lost privacy and sociability. Successful privacy and individualism depends upon functioning sociability, reflecting the 'twin ideals' of domestic privacy and social connectedness, and for tower blocks this implied a symbiosis between high-rise interiors and mass housing estate exteriors, both of which we have examined here. The design and functional form of high-rise blocks and estates, with essential elements of communality in and around the blocks, and yet sparse provision for sociability on the estates, was shown to be deficient as soon as social balance and sufficient management and maintenance were lost. In those circumstances, it is not surprising that social anxiety and social withdrawal became more prevalent over time, representing in a way the 'symbolic violence' of post-war high rise.[8]

This is partly a product of residualisation as predominantly defined in terms of the changing role of social housing and reflected in allocation policies and priorities.[9] As the constituency of residents altered with residualisation in the late 1970s and early 1980s, attitudes towards the communities that had grown up in blocks and on estates shifted markedly. Reflecting the broader interpretation of residualisation,[10] our respondents identified the gradual decline of residents' social responsibility and civility and of the council's investment in the maintenance and upkeep of blocks; reciprocal cleaning routines broke down and essential elements of the infrastructure such as lifts, stairwells and rubbish chutes were no longer given the attention they required. The combination of social and physical challenges within the blocks and on the estates, caused those who could do so to leave and many of those who stayed to socially withdraw in the worst cases.

The consequences of the residualisation of social housing, and of high rise in particular, also reveal a second symbiosis, that between internal (within estates) and external (within society) processes of respect, status and stigma. As people experienced social change within their own high-rise blocks and estates, with increasing numbers of vulnerable co-residents with multiple needs, some engaging in antisocial behaviour without sufficient local supervision and management, so residents not only socially withdrew, but also faced losing respect for themselves and others, the two being intimately linked.[11] In an attempt to retain self-respect, social distancing occurred within tower blocks and estates, such disengagement serving to make the attainment of sociability more difficult. The external, societal turn against modernist high rise, its loss of status from utopian future to dystopian reality, and its association in the public's mind with poverty and incivility, caused the loss of respect and empathy for high-rise residents,[12] the long-term stigmatisation of high-rise estates,[13] and reinforced the internal processes which eroded self-respect and sociability. The narrative of decline reported by residents themselves is a way of preserving the memory of a respectable past within high rise, in the face of such external stigma.[14]

Another key finding concerns the location and environment of the high-rise blocks. Estates located on the city's periphery were, from the very beginning, less successful than those closer to transport links and other amenities. The absence of essential services within walking distance or a bus journey had negative consequences for individual wellbeing (and especially for women) and for community cohesion. The design and planning of outdoor space was important as it not only affected people's experience of negotiating everyday tasks but it also influenced residents' perceptions of the area more generally; poor planning provision undermined people's need 'to feel that they belong somewhere'.[15] The exception to this were children. While adults fretted about the lack of designated play facilities on many estates, memories of childhood in the multi-storey flats tend to emphasise the freedom and creativity the estates and, in some cases, the surrounding natural and built environment facilitated.

Finally, we argue that if we are to understand high-rise estates we have to understand the people who live in them and the stories they tell about them. While external observers tended to see only the decline of estates and regard the physical deterioration as a signifier of failure, some residents' accounts tell stories of communal adaptation, stressing neighbourly relations and community belonging through simple everyday interactions. Although many people moved away from high rise in due course, some remained and of course others continued to be allocated to the blocks. Those people often sought to make the best of their situation. This perhaps helps to explain why, when high-rise blocks are identified for demolition, some residents express dismay and a desire to stay.[16]

Our oral history interviews have revealed that in contrast to the 'satisfaction' recorded by the majority of Jephcott's respondents in the 1960s, for some residents the initial material advantages of high-rise flats were quickly countered by the decline of the estate. Change often occurred quickly and the causes of the deterioration lay not only in the design but in the failure to maintain the physical and social environments which caused people to retreat to the privacy – or isolation – of their flats. But while a recent study has demonstrated that people's feelings of positive wellbeing are closely associated with the identification of the home 'as a haven, as a locus of autonomy and as a source of status', other factors detract from these benefits including the neighbourhood context.[17]

For the overwhelming majority of residents who were rehoused in the 1960s, the high flat was merely one stage in a housing journey that took them to alternative social housing or to private rented accommodation or owner occupation elsewhere in the city at a later date. The longer-term perspective permits us to think about high rise in this context – at least before residualisation altered the constituency of some blocks and brought about a much more fluid population. Conversely, where blocks contained a more stable population – and these tend to be those blocks of better design quality – one can point to more functional communities within the blocks as the example of Mrs Thallon and her neighbours discussed in Chapter 4 illustrates.[18] It is important to recognise that success existed alongside failure. For every Red Road or Queen Elizabeth Square there was a Moss Heights or Anniesland Court.

In addition to helping us understand change, and when that change occurred, our study has illuminated aspects of high-rise living rarely discussed or deemed worthy of attention. Given the importance of the home to post-war conceptions of wellbeing and contentment as well as official discourses on post-war reconstruction of the nation through regeneration of the population, we crossed the threshold to learn how people fashioned homes from their flats, negotiated the new communality in their block and on their estate. Memories of sunbathing on the veranda are juxtaposed – sometimes in the same interview – with stories of struggling with a pram when the lift broke down or encountering threatening behaviour in the stairwells. The everydayness of many of these observations should not detract from their significance. When one male resident articulated his fears about living high in the 1960s by explaining that lift failures meant he was unable to take his dog for a walk, we can both empathise and better understand how the design of high flats affected the most banal of activities.[19] And when we hear Jephcott's respondents expressing their concerns about the difficulties of drying the washing, the absence of play spaces for children or of communal facilities for adults, we can intuit what they regarded as basic amenities for a successful neighbourhood. Cosmetic changes to the physical appearance of many high-rise blocks in the city conceals a longer-term failure to enhance the environments in which they are located and helps us understand why, in Helen's words, 'you are safe from everybody but that's not a way to live'.[20]

All of which marks out a useful role for the social historian of Glasgow's high-rise revolution. Residents' personal histories supply evidence which might be used to question complacent academic assumptions regarding the inevitable failure of high-rise communities, and in this way, a revisionist social history of the multi-storey estate might feed into and inform policy discussions on any future national house-building programme. There are lessons to be learnt about how high-rise estates were designed, delivered, managed and maintained in the past which remain relevant to high-rise developments today and in the future. More broadly, however, in the wider public debate about contemporary housing problems, the case of multi-storey housing has value in promoting a 'critical public history' which recognises how processes of social identity and hierarchy continued to pervade our habits of thought and ways of seeing from the post-war years to the present day.[21] Through this critical public reflection, undertaken in collaboration with those who lived and still do live in high-rise flats. we might redefine the identity of high-rise communities, re-situating them within popular memory, while gaining a more complex understanding of the path leading us to the present.

Notes

1 Go-Well, 'The effects of high-rise living within social rented housing areas in Glasgow' (Briefing paper 11, 2011), www.gowellonline.com/assets/0000/0553/Briefing_Paper_11.pdf (accessed 11.12.2019).

2 *Housing in 20th Century Glasgow: Documents 1914–1990s* (Glasgow, 1996), p. 156.
3 Hazley *et al.*, 'People and their homes'.
4 Go-Well, 'The effects of high-rise living'; Kearns *et al.*, 'Living the high life'; Ade Kearns, Rosemary Hiscock, Anne Ellaway, Sally McIntyre, '"Beyond four walls". The psycho-social benefits of home: evidence from West Central Scotland', *Housing Studies* 15:3 (2000), pp. 387–410.
5 Go-Well, 'The effects of high-rise living', p. 3.
6 Lawrence, *Me Me Me,* p. 232.
7 Lawrence, *Me Me Me,* p. 233.
8 Lawrence, *Me Me Me,* p. 235.
9 Pearce and Vine, 'Quantifying residualisation'.
10 Forrest and Murie, 'Residualization and council housing'.
11 Richard Sennett, *Respect: The Formation of Character in an Age of Inequality* (Penguin, London, 2003).
12 J. Bannister and A. Kearns, 'Tolerance, respect and civility amid changing cities', in A. Millie (ed.), *Securing Respect: Behavioural Expectations and Anti-Social Behaviour in the UK* (Policy Press, Bristol, 2009), pp. 171–91.
13 Kearns *et al.*, 'Notorious places'.
14 Barry Hazley, Ade Kearns, Valerie Wright, Lynn Abrams, 'Place, memory and the British high-rise experience: negotiating social change on the Wyndford Estate, 1962–2015', *Contemporary British History* (forthcoming).
15 Lawrence, *Me, Me, Me,* p. 234.
16 For example, on the announcement that High-rise blocks in Irvine, a town south of Glasgow, were identified for demolition, some residents expressed their desire to remain. www.bbc.co.uk/news/av/uk-scotland-50672877/is-high-rise-life-on-its-way-out-in-scotland (accessed 11.12.2019).
17 Kearns *et al.*, 'Beyond four walls'.
18 In the Netherlands it has been shown that occupancy was the crucial factor for the performance of high-rise blocks. See van Kempen and Musterd, 'High-rise housing reconsidered'.
19 UGA, DC127/1/1-10/1: Dalmein Court.
20 Interview with Helen (Gorbals, b.1954), 2015.
21 John Tosh, *Why History Matters* (Macmillan, Basingstoke, 2008), esp. chap. 7.

Bibliography

Abrams, Lynn, Barry Hazley, Valerie Wright, Ade Kearns, 'Aspiration, agency and the production of new selves in a Scottish new town, c.1947–c.2016', *Twentieth Century British History* 29:4 (2018), pp. 576–604.

Abrams, Lynn, Linda Fleming, Barry Hazley, Valerie Wright, Ade Kearns, 'Isolated and dependent: women and children in post-war social housing in Glasgow', *Women's History Review* 28:5 (2019), pp. 794–813.

Attfield, Judith, 'Bringing modernity home: open plan in the British domestic interior' in Irene Cieraad (ed.), *At Home: An Anthropology of Domestic Space* (Syracuse University Press, New York, 1999), pp. 73–82.

Attfield, Judith, 'Design as a practice of Modernity: a case for the study of the coffee table in the mid-century domestic interior', *Journal of Material Culture* 2:3 (1997), pp. 267–89.

Attfield, Judith, 'Inside pram town: a case study of Harlow house interiors 1951–1961', in Judith Attfield and Pat Kirkham (eds), *A View from the Interior: Feminism, Women and Design* (Women's Press, London, 2nd ed., 1995).

Attfield, Judith, 'The tufted carpet in Britain: its rise from the bottom of the pile', *Journal of Design History*, 9:3 (1994), pp. 205–16.

Attfield, Judith, *Bringing Modernity Home. Writings on Popular Design and Material Culture* (Manchester University Press, Manchester, 2007).

Attwood, Lynne, *Gender and Housing in Soviet Russia: Private Life in a Public Space* (Manchester University Press, Manchester, 2010).

Bannister, Jon and Ade Kearns, 'Tolerance, respect and civility amid changing cities', in A. Millie (ed.), *Securing Respect: Behavioural Expectations and Anti-Social Behaviour in the UK* (Policy Press, Bristol, 2009), pp. 171–91.

Bartie, Angela, 'Moral panics and Glasgow gangs: exploring "the New Wave of Glasgow Hooliganism", 1965–1970', *Contemporary British History* 24:3 (2010), pp. 385–408.

Becker, F.D., 'The effect of physical and social factors on residents' sense of security in multi-family housing developments', *Journal of Architectural Research*, 4 (1975), pp. 18–24.

Boughton, John, *Municipal Dreams: The Rise and Fall of Council Housing* (Verso, London, 2018).

Brown, Callum G., 'Popular Culture and the Continuing Struggle for Rational Recreation' in T.M. Devine and R.J. Finlay (eds) *Scotland in the Twentieth Century* (Edinburgh University Press, Edinburgh, 1996).

Bruce, R., First Planning Report to the Highways and Planning Committee of the Corporation of the City of Glasgow, Corporation of the City of Glasgow (Glasgow, 1945).

Burbridge, M., *High Density Housing: A Social Perspective* (MHLG, London, 1969).

Castlemilk History, *The Big Flit: Castlemilk's First Tenants* (Castlemilk, 1990).

Cheadle, Tanya, 'Music hall, "mashers" and the "unco guid": competing masculinities in Victorian Glasgow' in Lynn Abrams and Elizabeth Ewan (eds), *Nine Centuries of Man: Manhood and Masculinities in Scottish History* (Edinburgh University Press, Edinburgh, 2016), pp. 223–41.

Clapham, David and Keith Kintrea, 'Rationing, choice and constraint: the allocation of public housing in Glasgow', *Journal of Social Policy* 15:1 (1986), pp. 51–67.

Cole, Ian and Robert Furbey, *The Eclipse of Council Housing* (Routledge, London, 1994).

Coleman, Alice, *Utopia on Trial: Vision and Reality in Planned Housing* (Hilary Shipman, London, 1990)

Collins, Chik and Ian Levitt, 'The modernisation of Scotland and its impact on Glasgow, 1955–1979: unwanted side effects and vulnerabilities', *Scottish Affairs* 25:3 (2016), pp. 294–316.

Conway, Jean and Barbara Adams, *The Social Effects of Living Off the Ground* (Department of the Environment, London, DOE Information Paper No. 9, 1975).

Cook, D.A. and H.G. Morgan, 'Families in high rise flats', *British Medical Journal*, 284: 6319 (1982), p. 846.

Crowson, N., 'Revisiting the 1977 Housing (Homeless Persons) Act: Westminster, Whitehall, and the homelessness lobby', *Twentieth Century British History*, 24:3 (2013), pp. 424–47.

Damer, Sean, '"Engineers of the human machine": The social practice of council housing management in Glasgow, 1895–1939', *Urban Studies* 37:11 (2000), pp. 2007–26.

Damer, Sean, *Scheming: A Social History of Glasgow Council Housing* (Edinburgh University Press, Edinburgh, 2019).

Davis, Angela, *Pre-school Childcare in England, 1939–2010* (Manchester University Press, Manchester, 2015).

Department of the Environment, *The Estate Outside the Dwelling: Reactions of Residents to Aspects of Housing Layout* (HMSO, London, 1972).

Doucet, Brian, R. van Kempen, and J. van Weesep, '"We're a rich city with poor people": municipal strategies of new-build gentrification in Rotterdam and Glasgow', *Environment and Planning A*, 43 (2011), pp. 1438–54.

Doucet, Brian, *Rich Cities with Poor People. Waterfront Regeneration in the Netherlands and Scotland* (Netherlands Geographical Studies 391, Utrecht, 2016).

Dunleavy, Patrick, *The Politics of Mass Housing in Britain, 1945–1975: A Study of Corporate Power and Professional Influence in the Welfare State* (Clarendon Press, Oxford, 1981).

Edwards, Clive, *Turning Houses into Homes. A History of the Retailing and Consumption of Domestic Furnishings* (Ashgate, Aldershot, 2005).

Fair, Alistair, *Modern Playhouses: An Architectural History of Britain's New Theatres, 1945–1985* (Oxford University Press, Oxford, 2018).

Forrest, Roy and Alan Murie, 'Residualization and council housing: Aspects of the changing social relations of housing tenure', *Journal of Social Policy*, 12:4 (1983), pp. 453–68.

Gibb, Andrew, 'Policy and politics in Scottish housing since 1945' in R. Rodger (ed.), *Scottish Housing in the Twentieth Century: Policy and Politics 1885–1985* (Leicester University Press, Leicester, 1989).

Gibb, Andrew, *Glasgow: The Making of a City* (Croom Helm, London, 1983).

Gibb, Kenneth, 'Transferring Glasgow's council housing: financial, urban and housing policy implications', *European Journal of Housing Policy* 3:1 (2003), pp. 89–114.

Gifford, Robert, 'The consequences of living in high-rise buildings', *Architectural Science Review* 50:1 (2006), pp. 2–17.

Glendinning, Miles (ed.), *Rebuilding Scotland: the Postwar Vision 1945–1975* (Tuckwell Press, Edinburgh, 1997).

Glendinning, Miles and Stefan Muthesius, *Tower Block: Modern Public Housing in England, Scotland, Wales, and Northern Ireland* (Yale University Press, New Haven, CT, 1994).

Glendinning, Miles and Stefan Muthesius, *Towers for the Welfare State: An Architectural History of British Multi-Storey Housing 1945–1970* (Scottish Centre for Conservation Studies, Edinburgh, 2017).

Go-Well, 'The effects of high-rise living within social rented housing areas in Glasgow' (Briefing paper 11, 2011), www.gowellonline.com/assets/0000/0553/Briefing_Paper_11.pdf.

Grindrod, John, *Concretopia: A Journey around the Rebuilding of Postwar Britain* (Old Street, London, 2014).

Hall, Peter, *Cities of Tomorrow: An Intellectual History of Urban Planning and Design* (Wiley-Blackwell, Oxford, 1988).

Hamlett, Jane, *Material Relations: Domestic Interiors and Middle-Class Families in England, 1850–1910* (Manchester University Press, Manchester, 2010).

Hanley, Lynsey, *Estates: An Intimate History* (Granta, London, 2012).

Harloe, Michael, 'The green paper on housing policy' in M. Brown and S. Baldwin (eds) *The Year Book of Social Policy in Britain 1977* (Routledge & Kegan Paul, London, 1978).

Harloe, Michael, *The People's Home: Social Rented Housing in Europe and America* (Blackwell, Oxford, 1995).

Hazley, Barry, Ade Kearns, Valerie Wright, Lynn Abrams, 'Place, memory and the British high rise experience: negotiating social change on the Wyndford Estate, 1962–2015', *Contemporary British History* (forthcoming).

Hazley, Barry, Valerie Wright, Ade Kearns, Lynn Abrams, '"People and their homes rather than housing in the usual sense"? Locating the tenant's voice in Homes in High Flats'. *Women's History Review*, 28:5 (2019), pp. 728–45.

Highmore, Ben, *The Great Indoors. At Home in the Modern British House* (Profile Books, London. 2014).

Hole, Vere (Ministry of Technology, Building Research Station), *Children's Play on Housing Estates* (London, HMSO, 1966).

Horsey, Miles, *Tenements and Towers: Glasgow Working-Class Housing 1890–1990* (RCAHMS, Edinburgh, 1990).

Housing in 20th Century Glasgow: Documents 1914–1990s (Glasgow, 1996).

Hurtwood, Lady Allen, *Planning for Play* (Thames and Hudson, London, 1968).

Jackson, John, 'Neo-liberal or third-way? What planners from Glasgow, Melbourne and Toronto say', *Urban Policy and Research*, 27:4 (2009), pp. 397–417.

Jacobs, Jane, *The Death and Life of Great American Cities* (Pimlico, New York: 1961).

Jennings, Hilda, *Societies in the Making: A Study of Development and Redevelopment Within a County Borough* (Routledge, London, 1962).

Jephcott, Pearl with Hilary Robinson, *Homes in High Flats: Some of the Human Problems Involved in Multi-Storey Housing* (Oliver & Boyd, Edinburgh, 1971).

Jones, Ben, 'Slum clearance, privatization and residualization: the practices and politics of council housing in mid-twentieth-century England', *Twentieth Century British History* 21:4 (2010), pp. 510–39.

Jones, Phil, 'The suburban high flat in the postwar reconstruction of Birmingham, 1945–71', *Urban History* 32:2 (2005), pp. 323–41.

Jury, A.G., *Housing Centenary: A Review of Municipal Housing in Glasgow from 1866 to 1966* (Corporation of Glasgow Housing Department, Glasgow, 1966).

Kearns, Ade, Elise Whitley, Phil Mason and Lyndal Bond, '"Living the high life"? Residential, social and psychosocial outcomes for high-rise occupants in a deprived context', *Housing Studies*, 27:1 (2012), pp. 97–126.

Kearns, Ade, Oliver Kearns, and Louise Lawson, 'Notorious places: image, reputation, stigma: the role of newspapers in area reputations for social housing estates', *Housing Studies*, 28:5 (2013), pp. 579–98.

Kearns, Ade, Rosemary Hiscock, Anne Ellaway, Sally McIntyre, '"Beyond four walls". The psycho-social benefits of home: evidence from West Central Scotland', *Housing Studies* 15:3 (2000), pp. 387–410.

Kearns, Ade., Valerie Wright, Lynn Abrams, Barry Hazley, 'Slum clearance and relocation: a reassessment of social outcomes combining short-term and long-term perspectives', *Housing Studies*, 34:2 (2019), pp. 201–25.

Keating, Michael, *The City that Refused to Die: Glasgow: The Politics of Urban Regeneration* (Aberdeen University Press, Aberdeen, 1988).

Kozlowsky, Roy, *The Architectures of Childhood: Children, Modern Architecture and Reconstruction in Postwar England* (Routledge, London, 20167).

Lawrence, Jon, *Me, Me, Me! The Search for Community in Post War England* (Cambridge University Press, Cambridge, 2019).

Maclennan, Duncan, *Housing in Scotland 1977–87* (Centre for Housing Research, Glasgow, 1980).

Maclennan, Duncan and Andrew Gibb, *Glasgow: No Mean City to Miles Better*, Discussion Paper 18. (Centre for Housing Research, Glasgow, 1988).

Maizels, Joan, *Two to Five in High Flats: An Enquiry into Play Provision for Children aged Two to Five Years Living in High Flats* (Housing Centre Trust, London, 1961).

Malpass, Peter and Alan Murie, *Housing Policy and Practice* (Macmillan, London, 1982).

Malpass, Peter, *Reshaping Housing Policy: Subsidies, Rents and Residualization* (Routledge, London, 1982).

Massey, Doreen, 'Places and their pasts', *History Workshop Journal*, 39 (Spring, 1995), pp. 182–92.

McCrone, Gavin, 'Urban renewal: the Scottish experience', *Urban Studies* 28:6 (1991), pp. 919–38.

Miller, Daniel, 'Appropriation of the state on the council estate', *Man*, New series 23:2 (1988), pp. 353–72.

Miller, Ronald and Joy Tivy (eds), *The Glasgow Region: A General Survey* (Edinburgh, 1958).

Miller, Ronald, 'The New Face of Glasgow', *Scottish Geographical Magazine*, vol. 86:1 (1970).

Ministry of Housing and Local Government, *Families Living at High Density* (London, 1970).

Ministry of Housing and Local Government, *Homes for Today and Tomorrow* (HMSO, London, 1961).

Moore, N.C., 'The personality and mental health of flat dwellers', *British Journal of Psychiatry*, 128:3 (1975), pp. 259–61.

Needleman, Lionel, 'The comparative economics of improvement and new building', *Urban Studies*, 6:2 (1969), pp. 196–209.

Newman, Oscar, *Defensible Space: Crime Prevention through Urban Design* (Collier Books, New York, 1973).

Newton, Tim and Charles Putnam (eds), *Household Choices* (Futures Publications, Middlesex, 1990).

Ortolano, Guy, *Thatcher's Progress. From Social Democracy to Market Liberalism through an English New Town* (Cambridge University Press, Cambridge, 2019).

Pacione, Michael, 'Renewal, redevelopment and rehabilitation in Scottish cities 1945–1981', in George Gordon (ed.), *Perspectives of the Scottish City* (Aberdeen University Press, Aberdeen, 1985), pp. 280–305.

Pacione, Michael, *Glasgow: The Socio-spatial Development of the City* (Oxford, 1995).

Pacione, Michael, 'The view from the tower: geographies of urban transformation in Glasgow', *Scottish Geographical Journal*, 125:2 (2009), pp. 127–81.

Pearce, Jen and Jim Vine, 'Quantifying residualisation: the changing nature of social housing in the UK', *Journal of Housing and the Built Environment*, 29 (2014), pp. 657–75.

Power, Anne, *Priority Estates Project 1982: Improving Problem Council Estates* (Department of the Environment, London,1982).

Power, Anne, *Hovels to High Rise: State Housing in Europe Since 1850* (Routledge, London, 1993).

Ravetz, Alison, *Council Housing and Culture: The History of a Social Experiment* (Routledge, London, 2003).

Ravetz, Alison and Richard Turkington, *The Place of Home* (Routledge, London, 1995).

Rodger, Richard (ed.), *Scottish Housing in the Twentieth Century: Policy and Politics 1885–1985* (Leicester University Press, Leicester, 1989).

Rogaly, Ben and Becky Taylor, *Moving Histories of Class and Community: Identity, Place and Belonging in Contemporary England* (Palgrave, Basingstoke, 2011).

Rudolph, Nicole C., *At Home in Postwar France. Modern Mass Housing and the Right to Comfort* (Berghahn, New York, 2015).

Saegert, S., 'Environment and children's mental health: Residential density and low income children', in A. Baum and J.E. Singer (eds), *Handbook of Psychology and Health* (Vol. 2), (Hillsdale, NJ: Lawrence Erlbaum, 1981), pp. 247–71.

Saunders, Peter, *A Nation of Homeowners* (Routledge, London, 1990).

Scottish Housing Advisory Committee, *Housing Management in Scotland* (Edinburgh, HMSO, 1967).

Sennett, Richard, *Respect: The Formation of Character in an Age of Inequality* (Penguin, London, 2003).

Sigsworth, E.M. and R.K. Wilkinson, 'Rebuilding or renovation', *Urban Studies*, 4:2 (1967), pp. 109–21.

Smout, T.C., *A Century of the Scottish People, 1830–1950* (Collins, London, 1986).

Taulbut, Martin, David Walsh, Gerry McCartney and Charles Collins, *Excess Mortality and Urban Change* (NHS Health Scotland, Glasgow, 2016).

Thomas, Andrew, *Housing and Urban Renewal* (Allen & Unwin, London, 1986).

Thomson, Matthew, *Lost Freedom. The Landscape of the Child and the British Post-war Settlement* (Oxford University Press, Oxford, 2013).

Torrington, Jeff, *Swing Hammer Swing* (Minerva, London, 1993).

Tosh, John, *Why History Matters* (Macmillan, Basingstoke, 2008).

Turkington, Richard, 'Britain: high rise housing as a "doubtful guest" ' in R. Turkington, R. van Kempen and F. Wassenberg (eds) *High-Rise Housing in Europe: Current Trends and Future Prospects* (DUP Science, Delft, 2004), pp. 147–64.

van Kempen, Eva and Sako Musterd, 'High-rise housing reconsidered: some research and policy implications', *Housing Studies* 6:2 (1991), pp. 83–95.

Walsh, David, Gerry McCartney, Charles Collins, Martin Taulbut and G.D. Batty, *History, Politics and Vulnerability: Explaining Excess Mortality in Scotland and Glasgow* (Glasgow Centre for Population Health, Glasgow, 2016).

Watt, S., 'Metamorphosis in the Gorbals' *The New Yorker*, 24 October 1959.

Watters, Diane, *Home Builders, Mactaggart and Mickel and the Scottish Housebuilding Industry* (RCAHMS, Edinburgh, 1999).

Willis, M., (Ministry of Housing and Local Government), *Living in Flats* (London, HMSO, 1952).

Willmott, Peter and Michael Young, *Family and Class in a London Suburb* (Penguin, London, 1960).

Wright, Valerie, Ade Kearns, Lynn Abrams and Barry Hazley, 'Planning for Play: Seventy years of ineffective public policy? The example of Glasgow, Scotland', *Planning Perspectives* 34:2 (2019), pp. 243–63.

Young, Michael and Peter Willmott, *Family and Kinship in East London* (Penguin, Harmondsworth, 1957).

Index